Rape

Rape

The Evidential Examination and Management of the Adult Female Victim

William M. Green, M.D.
University of California, Davis
School of Medicine

Lexington Books

D.C. Heath and Company/Lexington, Massachusetts/Toronto

Every effort has been made to ensure that drug dosage schedules and indications are correct at time of publication. Since ongoing medical research can change standards of usage, and also because of human and typographical error, it is recommended that readers check the *PDR* or package insert before prescription or administration of the drugs mentioned in this book.

Library of Congress Cataloging-in-Publication Data
Green, William M.
  Rape: the evidential examination and management of the adult female victim

  Bibliography: p.
  1. Rape victims—Medical examinations. 2. Rape
victims—Medical care. 3. Rape victims—Mental
health. 4. Rape victims—Services for. I. Title.
RA1141.G74 1988   362.8′83   88-45224
ISBN 0-669-19412-3 (alk. paper)

Published simultaneously in Canada
Printed in the United States of America
International Standard Book Number: 0-669-19412-3
Library of Congress Catalog Card Number 88-45224

The paper used in this publication meets the minimum requirements of American National Standard for Information Sciences—Permanence of Paper for Printed Library Materials, ANSI Z39.48-1984. ∞™

88 89 90 91 92 8 7 6 5 4 3 2 1

Contents

Figures

Tables

Preface and Acknowledgments

Confronting uncertainty is an integral part of health care delivery. Any patient can be a puzzle and any clinical encounter can offer mysteries. Clinicians spend years learning and developing strategies for problem-solving to reduce uncertainty and resolve unknowns. Indeed, it is these challenges to one's training and experience that make the practice of medicine such a stimulating and provocative endeavor. However, when presented with a conundrum for which adequate skills and tools are lacking, excitement quickly transforms into anxiety.

For many clinicians, a good example of this scenario is the task of evaluating the rape victim. Unfamiliarity with the special psychological needs of the victim, the unique aspects of the sexual assault history, the subtleties of the exam, and the techniques for evidence collection and preservation was as troubling for me as it seemed to be for most of my emergency department colleagues. These feelings of being unprepared and ill-equipped for dealing face to face with the victim escalated exponentially with my first trip to court as an "expert" witness in sexual assault. Thus motivated, I was determined to know more about evaluating and managing sexual assault before I examined the next victim or received the next subpoena. With the unanimous support from the division chief and fellow faculty members I agreed to compile a brief report on the evidential examination of rape.

I quickly discovered that the knowledge base for sexual assault evaluation was fragmented among the literatures of medicine, law, psychology, social work, forensic science, and criminal justice. I could find no single, comprehensive reference that adequately addressed all the major facets. As I collected resources regarding the various aspects of the problem I became acquainted with a number of individuals from other disciplines (district attorneys, police officers, psychotherapists, criminalists, and rape crisis workers), each of whom offered unique perspectives and expertise about sexual assault. They shared with me not only their knowledge and experience but also their frustration. Each discipline seemed to be primarily involved with its own separate piece of the sexual assault problem. The consensus that emerged was that each perceived a need to more fully understand the roles played by the others to more effectively aid the victim. All enthusiastically welcomed the prospect of a single volume resource describing the primary components in the evaluation and management of the rape victim. It is my hope that this book will help bridge the gaps among the many different professionals who are responsible for assessing and helping the rape victim.

This project would never have achieved fruition without the support, encouragement, and efforts of many people. Wayne Ordoz and Ken Peterson from the Sacramento County District Attorney's Office taught me much about the practical realities of investigating and prosecuting rape. Gary Goodpaster, associate dean of the University of California, Davis Law School, generously gave considerable time to review, critique, and discuss the material on the legal aspects of sexual assault. Joe Tupin, M.D., professor of psychiatry and medical director of the University of California, Davis Medical Center, helped me gain a better understanding about the psychodynamics of both the victim and the assailant. Niel Flynn, M.D., associate professor in the Division of General Medicine at the University of California, Davis Medical Center, reviewed and assisted in the compilation of the material on the treatment and prophylaxis of sexually transmitted diseases. My friends Gary Stewart, M.D., and Felicia Stewart, M.D., from Planned Parenthood of Sacramento Valley, offered not only their considerable expertise on postcoital contraception but also a large dose of encouragement.

I would like to acknowledge special gratitude to George Sensabaugh, Ph.D., professor of Forensic Sciences and Biomedical Sciences at the University of California, Berkeley, who spent many hours reviewing and guiding the revisions of the chapter on the forensic evaluation. His assistance went far beyond specific technical expertise, however. George's vast experience as author, scientist, and researcher, combined with his superlative teaching skills and gentle style, facilitated and supported this project in ways that cannot be measured. I must also express my deepest appreciation to Charles J. Fisher Jr., M.D., former chief of the Division of Emergency Medicine and Critical Care at the University of California, Davis Medical Center. His foresight and personal commitment to help create this book were invaluable. When Chuck left the University of California, Davis, to assume the chairmanship of the Department of Emergency Medicine and Critical Care at Case Western Reserve, he passed the baton to Robert W. Derlet, M.D. Bob shared Chuck's belief in the importance of this project and resolutely supported its completion. Without Chuck Fisher and Bob Derlet, this work would not have been written.

Lastly, I wish to thank Susannah Morey, Gilda Garcia, Bobbi Erickson, Carole Thompson, and Connie Chan. Their dedication, professionalism, and patience during the preparation and editing of the manuscript are greatly appreciated.

1
Introduction

F ew crimes in our society are more devastating—physically and emotionally—than sexual assault. The rape victim is often confronted with a terrifying array of threats, intimidation, and brutality. Fear of death is almost uniformly reported as the primary feeling during the attack. Rape is far more than a sexual act; it is a profound and violent insult to the body and the psyche. The person who has survived such a harrowing experience is left with a very special set of problems and needs. Regrettably, the medical and criminal justice systems have not always responded optimally. Prejudice, misconception, and myth still shroud the sexual assault victim.

The incidence of reported rape cases has been escalating at an alarming rate. During the last two decades sexual assault has been the fastest-growing violent crime in America.[1, 2, 47, 53, 56] According to Federal Bureau of Investigation statistics, a national total of 15,560 forcible rapes (completed or attempted rape by force) came to the attention of authorities in 1960.[56] The calculated occurrence rate was 17 cases per 100,000 women. By 1970 the number of reports had more than doubled to 37,270 rapes, or 36 per 100,000 females. In 1980, 82,088 complaints were filed, with rape reported by 71 out of every 100,000 women. Viewed from a different perspective, in 1980 police departments nationwide learned of a new sexual assault every 6.4 minutes.

Distressing as these statistics are, they represent only the tip of the iceberg. Most knowledgeable authorities agree that rape is the most underreported violent crime.[1, 7, 9, 15, 19, 34, 41, 53, 56] Accurate data is lacking, but most experts believe that far fewer than 50

percent of all sexual assaults are ever reported and many speculate
that the actual figure may be as low as 10 percent.

A variety of factors is operational on victim decision-making.
Fear of reprisal may be a potent deterrent. Embarrassment and
humiliation undoubtedly prevent many women from contacting
police. From the victim's standpoint, the witness stand may be the
instrument of a character assassination that can portray the victim
in a worse light than the defendant. The stigma of being raped and
the societal assumption of complicity often create intense feelings of
guilt that decrease the likelihood of a formal complaint being filed.
The disappointing figures related to arrest and conviction of rapists
offer little encouragement to the victim who is weighing the personal risks and sacrifices against her chances for obtaining justice.

The victim who makes the commitment to proceed against her
attacker presents a multifaceted emergency. Medical needs include
prompt attention to physical injuries (which may be life-
threatening), and careful documentation of all objective signs of
trauma (however subtle), which may be crucial to corroboration of
later testimony. Evaluation for and prevention of unwanted pregnancy and sexually transmitted disease are essential aspects of
complete medical care. The profound psychological impact of the
assault may be the most damaging and least obvious injury. The
clinician must understand the psychodynamics of the rape victim
and be prepared to help minimize emotional stress in the acute
situation and then make the appropriate referral. The interaction
between the patient's medical and legal needs creates an encounter
unique in the practice of clinical medicine. A variety of medical-legal
issues must be addressed and managed with meticulous technique
and compulsive attention to detail.

There seems to be an inherent reluctance among health care
providers, especially physicians, to become involved in the evaluation or treatment of rape victims. Few residency programs provide
the necessary training and skills to deal humanely and expertly with
this special group of patients. Many physicians who must care for
sexual assault victims do so grudgingly and with suspicion. Unfamiliarity with the details of evidence collection and preservation,
apprehension about the potential inconvenience and harassment of
a courtroom appearance, and ignorance about the true nature of the

crime and its victims are all factors that contribute to the pervasive negative attitude of the medical community.

The upsurgence of the feminist movement, which began in the early 1970s, has been a powerful social and political force that has greatly enhanced public awareness about rape. A more realistic understanding of the crime and the plight of its victims has improved the sensitivity of medical, legal, and law enforcement personnel who deal with sexually assaulted women. In many states, lobbying efforts by feminist groups have been pivotal in the passage of rape reform legislation. The movement can be justifiably proud of the fact that more reformation (both legislative and judicial) has occurred in the last fifteen years than ever before.

Enlightenment requires knowledge, understanding, and an open mind. The discussion that follows is an attempt to provide some insight into the complexities of the medical-legal evaluation and management of the sexual assault victim. The focus is the adult female who has been raped. Child molestation and sexual assault of the adult male are serious problems but beyond the scope of this report. A considerable amount of data and opinion about rape has been published in the medical and legal literature. Historical perspective and current thinking are reviewed and salient points underscored to assist all professionals in dealing more effectively with the sexual assault victim.

2
Historical Perspectives and Legal Issues

The word "rape" stems from the Latin "rapere," to take by force.[53] Since prehistoric times women have been justifiably fearful of the threat of rape. For centuries women have been considered mere chattel, subject to being bought, sold, bartered, or wagered. Forcible abduction and marriage was a long-standing and acceptable method of acquiring women. Legal limits on this activity probably first appear in ancient Babylonian and Mosiac Law, in which capture of females was only allowed if the women came from outside the tribe.[59] If the desired woman was inside the tribe, proper payment was required for legal possession. The code of Hammurabi, perhaps the most famous ancient legal doctrine dating back to about two thousand years before Christ, held that a woman had no independent status.[39] A female was either a virgin belonging to the house of her father or a maried woman belonging to the house of her husband. According to the code, if a virgin was raped she was guiltless and the man was put to death. If a wife was raped she was assumed to share the guilt with the attacker; both were thrown into the river. The husband was given the prerogative of saving his wife. The code thus provided on the one hand the first legal guidelines and punishment for the crime of rape and on the other hand the foundation for one of the basic myths about rape which tenaciously survives to this day: that the victim is in some way, or to some extent, a willing participant in the crime.

It was common practice in the middle ages for ambitious men to engage in "stealing an heiress" by abduction and marriage to gain property.[59] Even though heiress stealing finally became a felony crime in the 1400s, feudal law gave little protection or status to women. The lord of the manor had the right to take the virginity of the bride of any of his vassals or serfs who didn't pay "redemption dues." In keeping with the antiquated notion that women were property, females in times of war have historically been treated as part of the booty when conquering troops collected the spoils of war.

The general definition of rape varies widely in the legal statutes and medical literature. Perhaps the most commonly encountered definition is:

> The unlawful carnal knowledge of a woman by force and against her will.[9, 14, 15, 18, 41, 139]

This description of the crime has survived essentially unchanged since it first appeared in English common law in Elizabethan times (18 Eliz. 1, c7, 1576). This four-hundred-year-old definition has been the foundation for most state laws pertaining to sexual assault of the adult female. According to traditional interpretation, four criteria must be met for a rape to have occurred. First, there must be a victim and that victim must be female and not the wife of the assailant. The second ingredient, carnal knowledge, connotes sexual intercourse with penetration of the female genitalia by the penis. Thirdly, there must be nonconsent to sexual contact by the victim. Lastly, there must be the use of force to overcome the victim's will to resist.

Unfortunately, the practical application of this ancient law has for generations embraced our patriarchal and misogynistic heritage. Male dominance of government and the judicial system has nurtured a variety of misconceptions, myths, and sexist attitudes toward women and sexual assault. The notion that rape is a crime fantasized by pseudovictims who harbor ulterior motives has stubbornly resisted change. Seventeenth century British jurist Lord Hale was probably the first eminent officer of the court to verbalize this sentiment when he stated:

> Rape is an accusation easily to be made and hard to be proved and harder to be defended by the party accused though never so innocent.[145]

The chauvinistic beliefs that women should be afforded only second-class citizenship and should remain in their "proper place" are anachronistic reminders of society's traditional view of women and marriage.

Before the widespread reforms of the 1970s and 1980s there were very few meaningful changes in the sexual assault laws. One important exception was the recognition that the use of fear or threat to achieve sexual intercourse was just as repugnant and unacceptable as using physical force. Despite the often stringent qualifications placed on the kinds of threats that could equate with physical force, the legal system's acknowledgment of this type of coercion was a significant step forward in the prereform era.

The first substantive revisions of laws regarding sex offenses began appearing in the early 1960s as many states adopted reformed criminal statutes based on the American Law Institute's Model Penal Code.[139, 165] Although blatantly sexist in portions, the Model Penal Code did incorporate some important changes that anticipated the more progressive reforms of the 1970s. For example, consensual homosexual conduct between adults was decriminalized and some sex crimes (but not rape) were written in gender-neutral terms. Objective definitions of sex crimes were introduced and a spectrum of distinct prohibited acts was developed. The resulting graded series of offenses was matched to a set of proportional and discrete penalties. All penalties were generally reduced.[139]

Despite these positive aspects, rape reform advocates found a number of the Model Penal Code provisions objectionable and outmoded. They argued that many of the formulations were based on the 1950s view that rape was a charge easily and frequently leveled against innocent men by scheming and vindictive women. The codification of the common law doctrines of prompt complaint and corroboration were favorable to the defendant. The spousal exemption was not only retained but, in some jurisdictions, extended to include unmarried cohabitants. The prior sexual history of the complainant was easily accessible to the defense. If the victim was a "voluntary social companion" or "previously permitted" the defendant "sexual liberties," the charge was reduced. Further, if the victim could be shown to be "sexually promiscuous," this was considered an adequate defense to some sex offense charges.[165]

Critics of the Model Penal Code contend that these provisions supported the misogynistic notion that consent ought to be presumed and its absence disproved by the prosecution.[139] Regardless of its drawbacks, the Model Penal Code has been an important springboard for many subsequent reforms in sexual assault law.

Since the early 1970s the feminist movement has enjoyed groundswell status as a potent social and political force. By 1980 every state had considered and nearly all had passed some form of rape reform legislation.[139] More changes in the laws pertaining to sexual offenses have probably occurred in the last fifteen years than in all of recorded history. This remarkable accomplishment is due in part to a public that is better educated about the realities of rape and the plight of its victims. Feminists are largely responsible for this national dialogue and the resultant changes in public opinion. In addition, a substantial grassroots lobbying effort by several well-organized women's groups has had a significant effect on the passage of rape reform statutes, despite the fact that state legislators are predominantly male.[139]

Each element in the legal equation of sexual assault has been subject to scrutiny by reformers. The principal objectives of rape reform legislation can be grouped into several categories: goals associated with redefinition of the offense and reorganization of the penalty structure, goals associated with the repeal of the spousal exemption, and goals associated with protection of the victim at trial. The difficult issue of consent is the thread that weaves together these various objectives.

Consent

In the abstract, consent appears conceptually simple as it relates to matters of sexual intimacy; either the individual assented to sexual contact, or did not. The search for consent in any particular case may, however, be far from straightforward. Ambiguity, contradiction, ambivalence, and misperception may render precise characterization of the incident impossible. As the vagaries of consent intertwined with the traditional attitudes and beliefs about rape, a standard of consent developed in American case law which, to the objective observer, suggested a woman could agree to intercourse with strangers or acquaintances under circumstances of coercion, humiliation, or brutality.[139]

The inquiry into whether consent had been granted included an analysis of the complainant's character, her prior sexual history, her propensity to consent, and her reputation for chastity. Because a defense of consent concedes the fact that sexual intercourse did take place between the parties at controversy and upon the occasion in question, the primary defense tactic has been to discredit the prosecution's evidence of nonconsent. Historically, this subjected the victim to aggressive cross-examination intended to assassinate her character. Reformers argued that such a consent standard put the victim, not the assailant, on trial. The common law traditions surrounding consent are, for many strategists, a major unresolved issue in the restructuring of sexual assault law.

The classical approach to the issue of consent in rape cases has been shaped by a number of erroneous assumptions. The nucleus of these misconceptions is a recurrent theme in sexual assault juris-prudence; namely, a fundamental skepticism toward the veracity and character of the complainant. Subsequently, a legal framework that is unique to rape has developed and has tended to formalize this basic distrust. For example, traditional wisdom has maintained that the victim's prior sexual history provides insight into her behavior and credibility. If she is found to be "unchaste," the defense will likely equate this "moral flaw" with a general disregard for truthfulness and further suggest to the jury that if she consented once, she is most likely to have done so again.

Another questionable premise is that the actions of the complainant invited or precipitated the assault. The suggestion of contributory behavior may color jury deliberation by focusing attention on victim activity related to common social encounters. Casual conversation with a stranger at a party, accepting a ride home from an acquaintance, dating, or even consensual petting do not and should not preclude a person's right to refuse intercourse.[164]

Realistic and effective consent should include several elements. Fundamental to the notion of consent is the protection of physical safety. The law has an obligation to protect society and the individual from the injurious acts of others. The law has historically rejected the premise that a person could assent to severe injury or mayhem. Correspondingly, when serious injury occurs in the context of sexual assault, the court presumes the absence of consent. As previously noted, threats of great bodily harm have come to be recognized as jeopardizing personal safety and thus invalidating any consent given under such duress. Modern interpretation has added threats against third parties as sufficiently dangerous to prevent effective consent. Some jurisdictions have gone a step further by defining the harm caused by rape to include emotional and psychological unrest.[139] The law generally presumes consent to be absent when intercourse occurs incident to another crime (such as robbery or breaking and entering) or when a weapon is used.[139, 164]

The second major element of consent is the protection of freedom of choice. The law protects the individual's right of sexual selectivity; that is, the right to say "no." Violation of this policy depends neither upon whether force was used nor upon the magnitude of the force. In cases where the application of force is extreme and intercourse is achieved by way of a brutal beating, the issue of consent is irrelevant since one cannot legally consent to grievous bodily harm.[164] In this situation, the protection of social wellbeing overrides the exercise of free will. The law does acknowledge some forms of injury and violence as consensual (such as surgery or contact sports) but requires the individual at risk to be fully aware of and take responsibility for the consequences of his or her consent.

A variety of sexual encounters can occur in which force is not at issue but free choice is infringed. The law recognizes certain circumstances that prevent the individual from legally exercising freedom of choice despite apparent affirmative motivation or lack of unwillingness. The California Penal Code (Section 261.6) offers a concise functional definition of consent as it applies to sexual assault:

> . . . "consent" shall be defined to mean positive cooperation in act or attitude pursuant to an exercise of free will. The person must act freely and voluntarily and have knowledge of the nature of the act or transaction involved.

All states place age restrictions on lawful consent. An underaged female is considered incapable of granting effective consent to intercourse regardless of her desire to do so. Because her immaturity and inexperience prevent proper awareness and acceptance of the consequences of such consent, she lacks the legal capacity to use free choice.

If the individual suffers from impaired mental faculties, her apparent consent is irrelevant because the law presumes her to be ill-equipped to comprehend the essential elements of such a free will decision. A number of vague terms appear in the statutes to describe these disabilities, including lunacy, insanity, feeble-mindedness, unsoundness of mind, and retardation.

Intoxication with drugs and/or alcohol is usually considered sufficient to disturb reasoning and impair the proper use of free choice. If the victim is asleep or unconscious, obviously free will cannot be invoked and consent is presumed to be absent. Sexual intimacy achieved through fraud or deception (such as a fraudulent marriage ceremony) is nonconsensual because such behavior deprives the victim of sexual choice despite the fact the victim was unaware of the invasion of rights when it occurred.[164]

Rape reform advocates have vigorously supported legislative efforts to statutorily define situations of nonconsent. When clearly drawn, these statutes help obviate the state's burden of proving the absence of consent by describing, in objective terms, circumstances or indicia of nonconsent.

The third task of a reasonable consent standard is to define and limit the scope of consent. The policies protecting personal safety and freedom of choice can be served more effectively if the law clearly sets the boundaries of injury to which an individual can consent. As discussed above, the law allows the individual to voluntarily place himself in some situations entailing the risk of injury, so long as the person comprehends and accepts the consequences. Prerequisite to this acceptance, however, is a realistic understanding of the degree of risk involved. Under most circumstances the law will not tolerate injury that is intentionally inflicted and is in excess of the risk the individual can fairly be said to have assumed.

The working law of rape offers little support to this concept of "limited consent." The most dramatic example of the legal system's failure to secure the limits of effective consent in matters of sexual assault is the continued vitality of the marriage defense to rape. The spousal exemption to rape prosecution is discussed in detail later.

The boundaries of consent may also be problematic when evaluating the implications of a given consensual act. If the prevailing consent standard fails to clearly delineate the specific behaviors encompassed with the consensual framework of an encounter, variations in interpretation may jeopardize the individual's rights. A prime example of this principle is the pervasive assumption that consent to any sexual contact (kissing, caressing, petting, etc.) automatically implies consent to intercourse. Objective and realistic analysis of these circumstances should refute this notion of cascading consent without endpoint. Currently, neither the law nor public opinion demonstrates much sensitivity to this aspect of the limited consent concept.

The fourth and most difficult aspect of any consent standard is the necessity of characterizing the nature and degree of coercion required to distinguish submission from consent. A recurring source of confusion has been the tendency of some jurisdictions to equate use of force and lack of consent. Under traditional formulations, the definition of rape usually included the phrases "without her consent" and "against her will." At first glance these may appear to be equivalent but careful analysis reveals subtle differences. The first phase implies only that the victim withheld active approval, while "against her will" connotes active resistance. Conceptually, resistance is simply a message to the actor that nonconsent is present. In the context of sexual assault, resistance has developed the additional implication of tangible evidence for the jury. Varying interpretation has led some courts to consider resistance as a distinct element in the crime.[164] Use of force by the assailant has historically been held as an important indicator of nonconsent and completes the triad of nonconsent—resistance—force. Understanding the complex interrelationships among these three elements in any given case may be a task of surpassing subtlety.

When consent is at controversy in a sexual assault case, the court must scrutinize the interface between overreaching or imposition by the actor and nonconsent by the victim. Inquiry into the victim's subjective state of mind or the perpetrator's perception of her state of mind may uncover a quagmire of ambivalence, guilt, ambiguous communication, and unconscious restructuring of the event in question. The intention of the perpetrator, historically an essential factor in the equation of criminality, is another important, but evasive, variable. Confronted with these often insoluble difficulties, courts have traditionally focused on objective manifestations of assailant force and victim resistance as the primary indicators of nonconsent.

In other areas of criminal law where nonconsent and force are potentially or theoretically at issue (such as assault or robbery), the law interprets consent so as to promote a policy of personal safety by focusing on the actions of the one who inflicts the harm rather than the behavior of the recipient. Clearly, in most cases of assault or robbery, consent is a moot point. However, when controversy exists, the court usually applies a "reasonable man" test which allows the victim's actions to be judged in light of all the circumstances.[164] The result is generally a low standard of force required to prove victim fear and therefore nonconsent. The law does not expect the individual to risk death or serious injury in defense of property or self.[164]

The law of rape has evolved along a different and unique pathway. The pervasive atmosphere of distrust that shrouds the sexual assault victim has had a significant ripple effect. A judicial tendency emerged in which the court focused more attention on the behavior of the victim than on the conduct of the assailant. With the credibility of the victim in presumptive doubt, the requirements for proof of force and resistance ascended to a level much higher than that required in cases of robbery or assault. Most problematic from the victim's standpoint was the exaggerated insistence on evidence of resistance.

In the search for an objective external standard by which to measure the elusive and subjective element of nonconsent, the court has come to rely heavily on the manifestations of victim resistance. Proof of resistance has traditionally been evidence that the victim screamed, fought back, attempted to flee, or engaged in some other overt behavior that demonstrated her nonconsent. When injuries are severe or a credible third-party witness is available, a defense of consent is not likely to be employed. When physical findings of trauma are absent, minimal or nonspecific skepticism escalates. Although physical trauma is not a statutory requirement to prosecute rape, it is functionally very important and is frequently a determinant in penalty assignment. Despite the exact provisions of the statutes involved, a sexual assault jury may informally demand some corroboration of the victim's account of the incident, especially some indication that she resisted. Resistance, in the minds of many jurors, is probably equated with injury.

Before the reforms of the 1970s, judicial interpretation of traditional consent standards often demanded proof of "utmost resistance" by the victim to substantiate her allegation of nonconsent. The "utmost resistance" requirement had two components: first, the quality and magnitude of the struggle must reflect the victim's physical ability to oppose sexual aggression; and second, her struggle must not abate during the encounter. Some case law examples illustrate the demanding nature of the requirement.

> A mere tactical surrender in the face of assumed superior force is not enough. . . . Resistance must be unto the utmost.
>   Moss v. State, 208 Miss. 531,536,45 so.2d 125, 126 (1950)

> The most vehement exercise of every physical means or faculty within the woman's power to resist the penetration. . . .[must] persist until the offense is consummated.
> Brown v. State, 127 Wis. 193, 199, 106 N.W. 536, 538 (1906)

When the law demands resistance be taken to this degree, the victim is placed in a very precarious position for two reasons. First, opposition, especially vigorous opposition, may provoke extreme aggression from some types of assailants and subject the victim to considerably more violence than if she had not resisted. If the law's intent is to protect citizens from harm, a statute requiring a victim to behave in ways that could reasonably result in a significantly increased risk of grievous injury or death seems counterproductive. Second, it would certainly seem a miscarriage of justice to excuse an assailant because a weak or fearful victim failed to protect herself with the dedication and ferocity the court might expect in order to meet an unspecified "utmost" standard.

The common law and some early derivative statutes did recognize some special circumstances that could moderate the extremeness of the prevailing resistance doctrine. Intercourse achieved by the intimidation or threat was considered rape if the court could be convinced that those threats produced a paralyzing fear of great bodily harm or death.[165] In keeping with the traditions of suspicion and focus on victim behavior, the court usually set demanding standards on the types and intensity of threat that could constitute rape and thus excuse the victim from her duty of "utmost resistance." In addition to fear of serious injury or death, the standard in some jurisdictions required that the risk be immediate and accompanied by the actor's apparent power of execution.[165] The Model Penal Code rejected this constricted approach to coercion by threat but apparently did agree with the concept that intercourse via threat was sometimes rape and sometimes not. The drafters' concerns seemed to center on the court's ability to separate coercion from bargain. What resulted was gradations of penalties based on the gravity of the threat. Coercion was considered absent if the court determined the threat to be "trivial or remote."[165]

The prereform attitudes toward coercion and sexual intimacy provoked many objections. Reformers continually asserted the inappropriateness and unfairness of emphasizing victim behavior over assailant conduct. Relying on the contemporary view that the true harm in rape is the violation of free choice and the affront to personal integrity, reform advocates rejected the notion that the impact of the crime could be ameliorated by finding that a coercive threat was implausible or that the assailant lacked the capacity to follow through. Overreliance on resistance evidence carries the liability of nonprosecution in situations where meaningful consent was in fact absent but application of force was not apparent. Reformers argue that while the analogy of resistance as the mirror image of consent may have a degree of intuitive appeal, it lacks validity in a number of circumstances. Victim resistance does not automatically produce obvious or severe injuries. Most rape victims do not sustain severe physical trauma. Certain findings or signs of injury in the sexual assault victim can be very subtle (as discussed in the examination section) and easily overlooked by an inexperienced medical examiner or police officer. Fear or threat may have immobilized the victim and effectively prevented resistance. Psychological considerations aside, reformers staunchly contend that the mere outward appearance of being "uninjured" should, in no way, imply consent.

Supported by progressive recommendations in the Model Penal Code and the efforts of rape reform advocates, modern courts are adopting a more lenient posture toward the types and degree of coercion that will prevent effective consent. Threats to harm, kidnap, or falsely imprison a third person or threats of future retaliation against the victim or another person are now considered sufficiently coercive to force submission (for example, California Penal Code, Section 261.6). Some jurisdictions presume coercion if the perpetrator holds a position of family or institutional authority over the victim; such authority, it is reasoned, is equivalent to force (for example, N.M. Stat. Ann., Section 30.9.13[/a]). A few foreign jurisdictions (such as Yugoslavia, Switzerland, Soviet Union) have gone a step further by enacting statutes under which economic coercion precludes effective consent to sexual contact.[164]

Perhaps the most progressive reform statutes are those in which the drafters have elected to restructure the law of rape without using the term consent. The Michigan Criminal Sexual Conduct Statutes [Mich. comp. laws ann. 750.520A to .520L], enacted in 1975, are considered by many to be the most important model for the reform of sexual assault law. In addition to such innovations as gender neutrality for all sex crimes and defining "criminal sexual conduct" without using the term rape, these statutes define, in specific terms, a spectrum of prohibited sexual activity without using "consent" or "resistance." To maintain focus on the conduct of the actor, force and coercion are defined in the context of a number of specific circumstances. Reform advocates herald these statutes and their approach as a major step toward better protection of the rights and wellbeing of the sexual assault victim.

Scope of the Crime and the Penalty Structure

The Elizabethan "carnal knowledge" definition of rape used by most states prior to the reforms of the 1970s has been justifiably criticized because it is both restricted and nonspecific. Original statutes limited the crime to a male perpetrator and a female victim. This notion denied equal protection to males who could be sexually victimized because of diminished mental capacity secondary to physical or emotional disability or were under the influence of intoxicating chemicals. The original laws also failed to acknowledge and provide safeguards against homosexual rape. In response to the constitutionally compelled right to equal protection most states have enacted gender-neutral sexual assault legislation.[143] The purpose of criminal sexual conduct laws should logically be to protect *all* citizens from unwanted sexual intrusions; preservation of "male only" rape statutes is not only in conflict with the Fourteenth Amendment but also bolsters social roles and stereotypes that are no longer acceptable.

Another serious defect in the common-law–based statutes is the lack of specificity in defining the crime. Carnal knowledge is generally interpreted as insertion of the penis into the vagina.[139] Rape reformers have long objected to this limited legal connotation of sexual assault. The Michigan Criminal Sexual Conduct Statutes provided the first major reform in this area by stating:

> Sexual penetration means sexual intercourse, cunnilingus, fellatio, anal intercourse, or any other intrusion, however slight, of any part of a person's body or of any foreign object into the genital or anal openings of another person's body, but emission of semen is not required.

Succinctly stated, the California Penal Code (Section 263) provides that:

> The essential guilt of rape consists in the outrage to the person and the feelings of the victim of rape. Any sexual penetration, however slight, is sufficient to complete the crime.

Reform objectives related to the redefinition of rape have, in many states, included attempts to specifically delineate and categorize each individual act in the spectrum of criminal sexual conduct. Concomitant to this has been the restructuring of the penalty system to define offenses in terms of degrees in order to establish gradations of punishment for prohibited acts. The Model Penal Code of the 1950s and early 1960s popularized the general reduction of sentences for sexual crimes. The theory behind such reductions was that juries had been reluctant to convict for rape when the penalty was often the same as for murder.[139] As previously discussed, the drafters of the Model Penal Code seemed concerned about the possibility of false complaints with inappropriately imposed punishment. Considerable controversy and little consensus exist today regarding the various proposals for reorganizing sexual assault penalties. Most reform states have reduced sentences for the more serious sexual offenses, anticipating greater willingness of judges and juries to convict.[139] This notion is based more on conjecture than on empirical evidence and further research is essential. In other jurisdictions reformers have advanced legislation that restricts judicial discretion in sentencing by mandating minimum penalties and statutory prohibitions on suspended sentences or probationary terms. This subset of rape reform advocates apparently perceives judges as more a part of the problem than part of the solution.

The controversy over restructuring of the penalty system exemplifies a fundamental misconception that has a bearing on almost all rape reform efforts. Most reform legislation has been drafted with the presumption that rape cases are disposed of at trial. A basic reality of the criminal justice system is that only a minority of cases actually go to trial despite the Hollywood image of the adversarial process. Most cases are not concluded in front of a jury but rather achieve disposition through the small-group dynamics of plea bargaining. The players in the group must face each other day after day and are able to exercise considerable informal discretion. This system is much less structured than the courtroom and subject to influence by a variety of institutional factors (court delays, personalities, individual perceptions of the other players) that have little to do with the particular characteristics of the case. Strategies used at trial may be quite different than those applied to the plea bargaining conference for the same case. The actual impact of rape reform legislation on this very significant portion of the criminal justice system is largely speculative. Some commentators feel it is reasonable to conclude that reform statutes have had some effect on plea bargaining with fewer settlements favorable to the defendant and perhaps more prosecutions for original charges.[166]

Statutory Rape

Another area with little national consensus is the question of the appropriate age for consensual sexual activity. Legislators have generally agreed that young children need to be protected from sexual abuse by adults, but the issue of consensual sexual activity between teenagers is very much unresolved.

Sixteenth century English common law specified ten as the statutory age of consent. Most early codifications of statutory rape laws in the United States also used the Elizabethan age of ten. Many states changed their age provisions several times and by the 1950s the majority of states no longer set the statutory age at ten.[139] Despite this trend, however, the Model Penal Code of the late 1950s and early 1960s still suggested ten as the statutory age for rape (first or second degree felony; Sections 213.1, 213.2). The drafters of the MPC have been criticized for being more concerned with avoiding false complaints and potential harassment of men than they were for protecting young females from sexual exploitation and abuse. On balance, it should be noted that the Model Penal Code did anticipate later reforms by defining a lesser offense than rape (third degree felony) under Section 213.3(1) (a) as "corruption of minors and seduction." Under this statute, a crime has been committed if the female is younger than sixteen years old and the actor is at least four years older. Using this formulation, mutually consensual sex was permitted if the female was between the ages of ten and sixteen and the male was fewer than four years her senior. If the female was over sixteen years old, sex could be consensual regardless of the age of the male partner.

Before the reforms of the 1970s, laws regarding sexual conduct with young persons evolved along two pathways. The first was the protection of young children (usually under the age of ten or twelve) from any sexual contacts with adults; consent by the parties or use of force were not elements in the crime; the acts were simply prohibited.[139] These laws generally had universal support and exist today as child abuse or molestation statutes. The second pathway focused on the sexual behavior of females in the age ranges between childhood and adulthood (usually ten-to-twelve to sixteen-to-eighteen years of age). This group of statutory rape offenses seemed to be directed at regulating the consensual sexual activity of young females. The variation in age limits from jurisdiction to jurisdiction and the fact that many states changed their age provisions several times attests to the long-standing social ambivalence and hypocrisy about this issue.[139]

The social objectives of statutory rape laws (that is, regulation of consensual sexual activity of certain age groups) are obviously quite different than those objectives addressed by statutes pertaining to either sexual abuse of children or forcible rape of adults. This dichotomy of goals has contributed to legal contradictions (especially in states where statutory rape was included in the principal statute defining forcible rape). Penalties for statutory rape were usually much less than those for forcible rape. In New Jersey, for example, the maximum penalty for intercourse with a female younger than sixteen was fifteen years; the maximum sentence for forcible rape of an adult female was thirty years.[139] Inconsistency of interpretation resulted in some judges' taking the position that maximum penalty was fifteen years for any intercourse (consensual or brutal attack) with a female younger than sixteen years old.

The uniqueness of statutory rape law, especially the fact a defense of consent could not be used, generated some special defense strategies. Undoubtedly there were cases in which fear of prosecution was used as a lever to force "shotgun" marriages to pregnant teenagers. A number of prereform statutes made specific references to "chaste females" or females of "virtuous character." The chastity of the victim became a component of the crime included in the state's burden of proof. Since protection of virginity was a traditional objective of statutory rape laws, a defense based upon the "unchaste" character of the victim was arguably logical. Under such statutes the prior sexual history of the victim was vulnerable to detailed examination by the defense. The chastity of the victim, however, had no relevance to prove the crime if force was used.

The "mistake as to age" defense developed as a rule of reasonableness to protect the defendant in situations in which the female was close to the statutory age of consent and because of appearance or other circumstances caused the male to believe she was old enough. The classic case, People v. Hernandez (61 cal.2d 529, 393P.ed 673, 39 Cal. RPTr.361, 1964), involved a seventeen-year-and-nine-month-old female living in a consensual relationship. She had told the defendant she was eighteen (the local statutory age of consent). The California supreme court held that the defendant's reasonable (albeit mistaken) belief that his partner was eighteen deprived him of the necessary criminal intent to sustain a conviction. Unfortunately, this defense was subject to abuse and applied to situations in which the "reasonableness" of the "mistake" stretched credibility. Delays between the event in question and the victim's eventual testimony in court compounded the problem because the jury could be asked to examine the female and speculate on her past appearance. Additionally, this defense could be used to impugn the victim's character by implying that she provoked a sexual encounter by using make-up or suggestive clothing. Thus kindled, misogynic or sexist attitudes among jury members could unduly burden the victim.

By the late 1970s many states had adopted some degree of reform in their statutes pertaining to age-related sex offenses.[139] While no state completely fulfilled the objectives of rape reform advocates, several noteworthy trends have emerged. Very few states still retain formulations that refer to the victim's chastity. Most reform statutes have expanded and specified the acts prohibited with young people. Correlative to this has been the development in most states of two or three graded offenses for sexual conduct with persons below specific ages.[139] Gender neutrality in the statutory language of some reform jurisdictions has extended protection against homosexual acts and sexual intrusions upon boys by adult females. A number of states adopted the Model Penal Code formulation and have decriminalized consensual teenage sex by defining the crime in terms of a maximum allowable age differential (usually three to six years) between the parties. Some jurisdictions have abolished or limited the mistake as to age defense.

Spousal Rape

Until the last few years one of the most enduring anachronisms in Western jurisprudence has been the legal bulwark that supported the right of a husband to forcibly rape his wife. This concept of the "spousal exemption" originated in English common law of the seventeenth century.[139–141, 157–162] Previously quoted British jurist Lord Hale legitimized and advanced this notion when he stated:

> The husband cannot be guilty of rape committed by himself upon his lawful wife, for by their mutual matrimonial consent and contract the wife hath given herself in this kind unto her husband which she cannot retract.[140]

It is significant that this statement was supported neither by citation nor by argument. It is interesting to note that Lord Hale is probably best remembered because of the number of witches he sent to the stake. Lord Hale's argument, which has come to be known as the "irrevocable consent" theory, draws sustenance from two points. First, when these words were written marriage vows were sacred, forever, and a legally binding contract. Once the vows were taken, the wife was assumed to have given permanent, full-time consent to intercourse with her husband under any and all circumstances. Her personal consent upon a specific occasion was irrelevant. In fact, refusal was grounds for divorce.

The second point concerns the relative roles of men and women in society and in marriage. Men were superior and dominant; women were basically property; the purpose of marriage was procreation. Rape laws of the middle ages were designed primarily to protect property rights; either the father's "property" and financial investment in the virginity of his daughter or the husband's "property" interest in sexual exclusivity with his wife. Traditional interpretation of rape laws argued that theft was the *sine qua non* of sexual assault. A husband, therefore, could no more be guilty of raping his wife than an owner could be guilty of stealing his own property. Obviously, early rape statutes favored male property interests rather than victimization interests of women.

As the basis for the spousal exemption, Hale's notion that

marriage creates contractual and irreversible consent has been harshly criticized in the legal literature.[141, 158, 161, 162] It has been argued that this theory would not survive the classical tests for an implied or expressed contract. The marriage contract is unique in that its provisions are unwritten, its penalties not specified and the terms of the contract are unknown to the contracting parties.[162] Further, an "objective manifestation of intent to agree," an essential ingredient in a valid contract, is lacking.[158, 162] The appropriate remedy for breach of contract is generally to sue for damages. The remedy of forced performance, as implied in Hale's theory, seems inconsistent with the spirit of the law.[158]

An additional flaw in the doctrine centers on the controversy over the definition of rape. If one accepts the contemporary and well-substantiated view that rape is a crime of violence, not an act of sexual passion, the consent theory becomes illogical. It is unreasonable to suggest that by taking marriage vows the woman automatically consents to a forced or violent sexual assault upon the whim of her husband.[161] If the state has a basic interest in protecting personal safety, the matrimonial consent theory appears inconsistent with this goal.

Another theory offered in support of the common law spousal exemption is based on the middle ages belief that a wife was her husband's chattel or property. Forced sex, therefore, was just another way that the "master" might choose to "use his property." Blackstone, the eighteenth century British legal scholar, advanced a corollary to this theory with the so-called "unity in marriage" or "unity of person" doctrine.[141, 161, 162] According to Blackstone, when a woman marries, her legal existence is suspended and her very being is absorbed by her husband; the husband is the only legal entity in the marriage. These "unity" theories have been used as a rationale for the marital rape exemption by arguing that a husband could not be guilty of raping himself. When scrutinized in the light of today's standards, these concepts are, at best, farfetched.

These attitudes that women are "nonbeings" or their husband's property have nearly disappeared from American jurisprudence.[161, 162] The trend in both statute and case law since the nineteenth century has been away from such discriminatory practices and toward a more equitable application of the laws.[161] Spousal immunity is the vestigial exception.

Despite the fact that the common law foundations for the spousal exemption today seem outdated and illogical, the rules tenaciously persist in most jurisdictions.[139, 140, 152, 158, 160] To explain its continued existence, modern authors have proposed some imaginative theories. The sparcity of legal or scientific support in the literature has spawned a series of arguments which, at some levels, may be intuitively persuasive but tend to overlap and rely on each other, rather than fact, for substantiation.

It has been suggested that marital rape is not a serious problem.[140] Quantitatively, this argument contends that spousal rape occurs too infrequently to concern the criminal justice system. The rarity of filed complains attests to the fact that in most jurisdictions the act does not constitute a crime. The women's movement, which matured during the 1970s, brought to light the violence that substantial numbers of women suffered at the hands of their husbands. A number of investigators believe that a significant portion of this abuse involves sexual brutality. For example, one study found that 37 percent of 325 battered wives reported also being sexually assaulted by their husbands.[140] Gelles, on the basis of his research, estimated that two million wives are battered by their husbands yearly.[152] He went on to estimate that 20 percent of these, or four hundred thousand cases a year, include forced sexual intercourse.

Proponents of the spousal exclusion claim spousal rape is qualitatively different (less severe and less damaging) than stranger rape. Interestingly, this theory draws support from the current view that the true evil of rape is not simply an attack on the vagina but rather an injury to autonomy and self-esteem. Since marriage decreases one's general expectations of personal autonomy, this theory maintains, the affront to the wife's autonomy is less in spousal rape than in stranger rape.[159] It follows, therefore, that spousal rape inflicts less harm. This series of inferences is not supported by any scientific data. To the contrary, current information is tending to suggest the opposite conclusion. Spousal rape may well be more damaging, both physically and emotionally, than stranger rape. The closer the relationship between victim and assailant, the greater the probability that the woman will resist and thus be subjected to physical violence.[140, 141, 143] Experience gathered from rape crisis centers indicates that marital rapes may involve some of the most significant physical abuse.[140, 141, 143]

The emotional and psychological trauma suffered by victims of sexual assault is now well-accepted. The notion that spousal victims experience less psychic harm than stranger rape victims is unsubstantiated. Sociological work suggests the opposite may be true.[143, 161] The basic nature of the marital relationship centers on mutual trust and consideration. Spousal rape betrays these values and strips the victim of an otherwise important resource (her husband) for support and recovery. The fear and humiliation suffered by all sexual assault victims is much less likely to diminish over time for the wife who has been raped by her husband. Two factors contribute to this ongoing fear and impaired self-esteem. First, the assailant usually remains in the relationship and in the home. Second, spousal rape, like wife beating, tends to be repetitive, leaving the wife in a constant state of apprehension and dread.[161] To compound matters further, the spousal victim may find herself in an economic dilemma in which she is forced to choose between financial support for herself and her children and freedom from the abusive environment.

Another defense for spousal immunity contends that the criminal law is an inappropriate forum for resolution and better alternative remedies are available. The first component of this argument advocates counseling and mediation as a solution and warns that criminal prosecution will lessen the likelihood of reconciliation.[141, 159, 161, 162] The flaw in this line of reasoning is the presumption that such a marriage is salvageable. A relationship that has deteriorated to a level of forced sexuality may well be beyond repair. This theory also ignores the gravity of the abuse already suffered and fails to address the dangerous potential of future abuse.[162]

The second level of this argument allows for the possibility of nonreconciliation but recommends civil litigation (divorce or legal separation) as a better alternative than criminal prosecution.[140, 141] Again, this solution fails to acknowledge the gravity of the act and implies that spousal rape is simply marital misconduct. The final thrust of this defense for the spousal exemption asserts that existing statutes for assault and battery should provide adequate protection and redress for the victimizied wife.[140, 141, 161] None of these "alternative remedies" serves the same personal and social values as criminal prosecution for rape. Lawmakers have traditionally recognized rape as a separate and more serious crime than assault and battery. Statutory classification of sex offenses, which have levied much harsher punishments for rape, reflect the greater psychological and emotional harm to the victim. Prosecuting a rapist husband for assault and battery unreasonably minimizes the consequences of the act and ignores the deterrent and educative functions of the law.

Probably the most classic justification for the preservation of the marital rape exemption is the longstanding fear that if eliminated, the flood gates would open and the criminal justice system would become clogged with the false accusations of spiteful and vindictive wives.[140, 141, 158, 160, 161, 162] The roots of this argument are not in marital rape per se but come from deep-seated misogynistic beliefs associated with forcible rape in general. Since the time of Lord Hale, female rape victims have had to meet a dual burden of proof. Not only must the victim prove her assailant is guilty, but she must also prove herself innocent of any complicity in the act. In most areas of sexual assault, reform legislation and a better-informed public have combined to discredit traditional beliefs about the inherent mendacity of women. In spousal rape, however, these attitudes seem to be especially well-entrenched.

Rebuttal to these arguments is multifaceted. First, there is no basis in fact that women lodge false rape complaints with any greater frequency than do victims of any other crimes.[140, 161] One unpublished study by the New York City Police Department (cited by Schwartz[140]) examined 2,046 rape reports in 1975 and determined that only 0.25 percent could be classified as "malicious." Second, it defies credibility to suggest a woman would casually subject herself to the social stigma of being raped and unnecessarily expose herself to the shame, humiliation, and intense public scrutiny experienced by the sexual assault victim. In fact, these negative features are undoubtedly contributory to the finding that rape is the most underreported violent crime in America.[1, 7, 9, 15, 53, 56, 158, 160] A vengeful wife bent on destroying her husband through a fabricated criminal charge could select a number of more productive alternatives since the acquittal rate for rape exceeds that of any other felony.[141, 158]

The third counterargument relies on the mechanics of the criminal justice system. In criminal law a number of oath-against-oath situations arise and in nearly every instance the investigatory responsibilities of the police and prosecutor, coupled with the inherent power of the judge and jury, are considered sufficient to determine the veracity of the allegations and to protect the innocent. Without any rational basis, lawmakers have historically considered spousal rape unique to the point of removing an entire class of potential victims from the protection of the law. It seems implausible to conclude that our system of jurisprudence will completely and utterly fail to operate in this one circumstance.

Another popular stance in support of the spousal exemption for rape revolves around two related problems—the burden of proof and the issue of consent. All rape cases are relatively difficult to prosecute and prove.[161] But marital rape presents some unique and challenging evidentiary problems. In nonspousal rape if consent is at controversy, the onus to prove its existence falls upon the defendant. The law presumes that marriage partners have, at least at some point, had consensual sexual relations. In marital rape, therefore, the burden of proof is shifted to the wife, who must present evidence to show that upon the charged occasion sex was different; she must prove she did not consent and was forced to have sex.

Proponents of the spousal exclusion have pointed out the pitfalls faced by the fact-finder in situations of vicissitudinous consent. Most problematic are the cases that lack any objective signs of trauma or violence; ultimately, the controversy is distilled to an "oath-versus-oath" encounter. Closely related is the concept of consensual ambiguity. It may be difficult, if not impossible, to draw a clear dividing line between begrudging acquiescence and forced compliance. Genuine but mistaken belief in consent is commonly offered as another potential obstacle to justice in spousal rape. Standard examples include the husband who engages in sexual activity with his sleeping or intoxicated wife and the circumstance in which the husband inappropriately interprets his wife's resistance as a ploy to enhance sexual pleasure. With such evidentiary hurdles to leap, advocates of a spousal exclusion warn that convictions for marital rape may at best be very difficult to secure and at worst may be unwarranted.

Both supporters and critics of the spousal exclusion tend to agree on the point that marital rape will be difficult to prove and convictions few.[140, 141, 161, 162] Critics argue, however, that many types of prosecutions are rare and arduous—treason, for example—yet society has determined that there are compelling moral and social reasons to retain such statutes on the books. In the District of Columbia v. Thompson [346 U.S. 100,117(1953)], the Supreme Court ruled that infrequent use of a law does not "bear upon the continuing validity of the law." The mere fact that a statute is seldom employed or that it engenders evidentiary problems are insufficient reasons to negate its existence.[160, 161, 162] Rape reform advocates also point out that to criticize a statute because it may be difficult to enforce fails to acknowledge the other important ancillary functions of the law.[140, 160]

Obtaining convictions is not the sole purpose behind criminalizing certain behaviors. The deterrent effect of the law, while aimed at a relatively small portion of the population (those who are potential offenders), has always been considered a substantial force in the criminal justice system. It can be logically argued that the vast majority of husbands do not and will not rape their wives; a small percentage of men do and will continue to sexually brutalize their spouses despite any number of legal prohibitions. The third group is the target. These are husbands who have in the past sexually abused their wives but perhaps will not again because of the risk of prosecution. A few well-publicized prosecutions for spousal rape may well pay long-term dividends to society far in excess of the incarceration of a handful of brutal husbands.

In addition to enforcement and deterrence, the law also performs important symbolic and educative functions. Since ancient times, the law has reflected the values and moral standards of a culture. Societal concepts of right and wrong have many origins but one is certainly the criminal law. In general, the public is more likely to view a given behavior as immoral if it is illegal. A statute that is clearly drawn, and in the common knowledge of the community, affirms the moral blameworthiness of the act, and helps define the boundaries of acceptable behavior. For some, the mirror image of this argument may be persuasive; if it is not illegal, it must be right. Opponents of the spousal exemption maintain that the preservation of such statutes fosters traditional, but no longer acceptable, attitudes and stereotypes of male dominance and women as chattel. In addition, this argument continues, a law that exempts a husband from rape charges carries the implication that society condones violence and sexual brutality if it is confined to the marital relationship.[140, 160]

The marriage defense to rape stirs debate on some important constitutional issues. Statutes that exempt a husband from criminal prosecution for sexually assaulting his wife create two classifications of women: married and unmarried. Married women, under these statutes, are denied some protections afforded to unmarried women. Critics of the spousal exemption argue that such dichotomous classifications fail to provide the equal protection guaranteed by the constitution. Support for this view has been extrapolated from Eisenstat v. Baird (405 U.S. 438 [1972]), in which the U.S. Supreme Court found unconstitutional a statute that prohibited the sale of contraceptive devices to single people but allowed sales to married persons. The court held that such discrimination based on marital status violated the equal protection clause of the Fourteenth Amendment.[143] The thrust of this ruling is that when two groups are exposed to an identical evil, the state must protect both equally; to deny protection to one group would represent "invidious underinclusion."

The spousal exclusion also raises questions and conflicts about constitutional rights to privacy. The Supreme Court first recognized the right to privacy in 1891 (Union Pacific Railway v. Botsford Co., 141 U.S. 250 [1891]). Current jurisprudence holds that individual privacy rights are fundamental and firmly rooted in the First, Fourth, Fifth, and Fourteenth Amendments.[141] Case law has helped define the scope and boundaries of these rights. Early Supreme Court decisions (Union Pacific Railway v. Botsford Co., cited earlier; Jacobson v. Massachusetts, 197 U.S. 11 [1905]) held that nonconsensual physical invasions infringed on individual privacy rights.[141, 143] Subsequent cases have expanded the coverage of the right to privacy to include certain personal decisions related to bodily functions and integrity. In Skinner v. Oklahoma (316 U.S. 535 [1942]), for example, the court found unconstitutional a state statute that authorized the involuntary sterilization of certain prisoners. They reasoned that the right to privacy included the fundamental right to procreation.

One of the most important cases of this type is Roe v. Wade (410 U.S. 113 [1973]), in which the court ruled the "right to privacy" to be "broad enough to encompass a woman's decision whether or not to terminate her pregnancy." Reproductive freedom and privacy rights were again at issue in Carey v. Population Services International (431 U.S. 678 [1977]). In this case the Supreme Court struck down a New York statute restricting the distribution of nonmedical contraceptives. The court concluded that an individual's right to privacy extends to the decision on whether to accomplish or prevent conception.[141] An important unifying theme that has emerged from these and related cases has been the court's insistence that when a statute interferes with the fundamental privacy rights of the individual, the state must demonstrate a "compelling interest" to justify the infringement. Further, the statute must be "narrowly drawn" to express only those legitimate state interests involved.[144, 143]

Rape reform advocates have found support for abolition of the spousal exemption in the Supreme Court decisions on abortion and contraception. A woman's right to bodily privacy and freedom from nonconsensual physical invasions are clearly in jeopardy when confronted by statutes that grant spousal immunity from rape prosecution. A related, but more theoretical, argument against the spousal exclusion can be made based on the court's findings in Carey. If the right to conceive is fundamental, the individual should have the right to prevent conception by using any available legal method. Abstinence from sex is an effective and legal form of contraception. To allow a husband to have intercourse with his wife (and thus potentially impregnate her) without her consent and against her will would seem to impermissibly burden the woman's decision about contraceptive choice and whether to beget a child.

Supporters of the spousal exemption have asserted the existence of "compelling" state interests of sufficient magnitude to justify overriding a wife's right to privacy. Maintaining marital harmony is the most common example.[141, 143, 159] This theory can be rebutted on several accounts. First, the origins of the exemption focus not upon concerns regarding marital harmony but on Hale's irrevocable consent doctrine. Further, the spousal exemption was spawned long before the recognition of a right to privacy.[141] Viewed in the light of modern jurisprudence, it is illogical to suggest that an antiquated and unsound common law doctrine should outweigh a fundamental constitutional right. Even if marital harmony qualified as a legitimate and compelling state interest, the spousal exclusion would fail the "narrowly drawn" test. It is, at best, improbable that the state's interest in matrimonial accord could be served in a relationship that has decayed to the point of sexual violence; thus, the state fails to express only that interest.

Some commentators have argued that elimination of the spousal exemption might actually impinge on another facet of privacy rights; namely, the fundamental right of marital privacy.[159] This theory asserts that the state has an interest in preventing public examination of marital intimacies and in promoting the private resolution of marital problems. An important foundation for the right of marital privacy is Griswold v. Connecticut (381 U.S. 479 [1979]). At issue was a state statute that prohibited married persons from using contraceptives. The court found the statute unconstitutional because it invaded married persons' rights to privacy by interfering with their decision to use or not use contraceptives. Without defining the scope of the right the court articulated the general right of marital privacy.

Advocates of the marital rape defense suggest that this general right may extend to the point of prohibiting state intervention into the marital relationship even if one spouse is sexually assaulting the other. Several Supreme Court rulings have helped clarify this controversy. The Griswold court concluded that marital privacy rights protected the couple from state invasion into *consensual* sexual behavior; this right does not interfere with the state's proper regulation of sexual misconduct.[143] In Eisenstat v. Baird (cited above) the court defined the right to privacy as an individual right. Marital privacy, they reasoned, was simply the combined privacy rights of each individual partner. Planned Parenthood v. Danforth

(428 U.S. 52 [1976]) struck down a statute requiring the husband's consent before an abortion could be performed on his wife. Because the state, according to Roe v. Wade (cited above), cannot prohibit first trimester abortions, the Danforth court ruled that neither can husbands. This decision not only confirmed the right to privacy as an individual right but also pointed out that when a conflict occurs individual privacy rights outweigh marital privacy rights. If the state was required to demonstrate a "compelling interest" to justify overriding marital privacy rights, it could offer the state's interest in protecting its citizen's fundamental rights to bodily privacy and freedom of procreation.

In view of the privacy rights, critics of the spousal exclusion contend that the only constitutionally sound rape laws are those that do not codify a spousal immunity from rape prosecution. The state has no compelling reason to protect the right of one spouse to rape the other. Any defense to rape that relies on marriage to the victim should be struck down because it must adversely affect the fundamental rights of personal bodily privacy and procreative autonomy.

Despite this collection of seemingly well-founded arguments in support of repealing the spousal exemption, less reform legislation has been enacted in this facet of sexual assault law than in any other. Even more curious is that during the reform process, some states actually extended the scope of the exemption to include unmarried cohabitants.[140] A few of these states went further by exempting "voluntary social companions." The extreme example was North Dakota[140] where an exemption to the Class A felony of Gross Sexual Imposition was extended to any defendant who has *ever* been granted "sexual liberties" with the victim. Predictably, such changes have been met by harsh criticism from reformers who advocate total elimination of the spousal exemption. These new statutes, they argue, not only affirm the vitality of an unfair and outdated doctrine but extend protection to areas never previously addressed by the common law.

Today, state statutes span a broad spectrum from total exemption to no exemption with a variety of partial exemptions covering the middle ground. By 1988 eighteen states had legislatively removed all forms of spousal immunity for rape.[196] Nineteen states currently retain some elements of spousal exclusion while thirteen states still support marriage as a defense for sexual assault.[196] Some of these complete spousal exclusions have been extended to protect a husband who is physically or legally separated from his wife.[196]

The lawmakers in California offered a unique approach to the problem by creating a separate crime for spousal rape. During its first two years on the books (1980–1981), the California statute (Penal Code, Section 262) was used twenty-four times.[140] Two of these cases were dropped but later replaced with murder charges; nine other cases were dropped by the prosecutor, primarily because of victim withdrawal or unwillingness to testify. Of the other thirteen cases, nine pleaded guilty or no contest, three were found guilty, and one was acquitted. The statutory changes in these few states are too recent and the data too limited to speculate about the overall effect such laws have on the problem of spousal rape.

Prior Sexual History

In the prereform era the complainant in a sexual assault case had just cause to be apprehensive about her day in court. From the victim's viewpoint, the atmosphere at trial was often one of suspicion and mistrust which focused more on the victim's behavior and character than on the crime committed. In many instances the victim seemed to be the one on trial; she had to prove to the court that she did not precipitate or solicit the act. Vulnerability was probably greatest in areas pertaining to the complainant's prior sexual history. Bullied, harassed, and humiliated by the defense attorney, many victims perceived the trial to be almost as degrading as the rape itself. Reformers argued that such conduct was not only unwarranted character assassination but also prejudicial and a clear infringement of the victim's privacy rights.

By the end of the 1970s most state legislatures apparently agreed, because forty-one states had passed some form of rape evidence statute.[139] These reforms, generically referred to as "rape shield" laws, are special evidentiary provisions that limit the admissibility of evidence of the victim's prior sexual conduct with persons other than the defendant.

To understand the genesis of rape shield statutes, it is necessary to explore the traditional view that advocates the relevance of the complaining witness' prior sexual conduct. Historically, the defense could offer evidence of the complainant's prior acts of consensual, nonmarital sexual activity with the defendant or with other men to show her "prior unchastity." Chastity in this context refers not to virginity but rather to the absence of sexual relations outside marriage.[163] If prior unchastity could be shown, the defense attorney would invite the jury to accept a series of inferences about the victim's veracity and conduct. The argument might proceed as follows: "unchastity" tends to imply a basic moral indifference that sheds doubt on the complainant's commitment to truthful testimony, which in turn should promote skepticism about her version of the event in question, especially the issue of her alleged nonconsent to sexual activity.

Until 1974, when it was striken by statute (Calif. Penal Code Sections 1127d and 1127e), a standardized California jury instruction in rape trials (former CALJIC No. 10.06) exemplified the traditional common law support for this theory:

> Evidence was received for the purpose of showing that the female person named in the information was a woman of unchaste character.
>
> A woman of unchaste character can be the victim of forcible rape but it may be inferred that a woman who has previously consented to sexual intercourse would be more likely to consent again.
>
> Such evidence may be considered by you only for such bearing as it may have on the question of whether or not she gave her consent to the alleged sexual act and in judging her credibility.

Prior sexual history (and its inferential offspring, "unchaste character") offered in this fashion falls into the category of character evidence. This area of the law is particularly complex and confusing.[163] In general, two sets of prohibitions regulate character evidence. The first type limits the occasions or purposes for which such evidence is permissible. Before rape shield reforms, character evidence in rape cases was usually introduced under either of two so-called "character theories." These related arguments (summarized by CALJIC 10.06) used inferential leaps to connect the complaining witness' prior sexual history to "unchaste character" and then to either impeach credibility or to advance the presumption of consent. Assuming character evidence may be used, the second category of prohibitions regulates the type or form of evidence that may be employed. The three most common vehicles for the introduction of character evidence are opinion evidence, reputation evidence, and evidence of specific acts or conduct.

Reformers have vociferously promoted a number of arguments against the use of the victim's prior sexual history. From the complainant's point of view, the demeaning and brutal methods often employed by the defense for the extraction of this information may create the experience of a second rape. Not only is this traumatic for the individual on the stand, but such testimony may also validate a form of community paranoia about the inherent perils of pursuing a sexual assault complaint. Although statistical support is lacking, reformers contend that such widespread beliefs contribute significantly to the fact that rape is the most underreported violent crime.[56]

The defense tactic of stacking inference upon questionable inference has raised many objections. Reformers reject the theory that prior consensual activity represents a moral flaw that precludes honesty and implies consent. The victim's "unchastity" sheds little, if any, light on the factual soundness of the defense. Character evidence is presented to show traits of character. Character traits are not neutral, objective facts; they are inferential, subjective assessments intertwined with the beliefs and moral judgments of the observer.

The system of trail by jury rests on the concept of societal judgment of the accused by his or her peers. These societal judgments will naturally reflect the views and value systems of the individual jury members. Sexist and misogynous attitudes toward rape victims are ubiquitous and deepseated. With this backdrop, reformers warn of the rich potential for jury misuse of prior sexual history data. The fear is that the jury will not rationally use the information within its intended purpose and context but will react emotionally to it and respond with an irrational verdict. In this view it can be argued that an acquittal does not necessarily mean the jury believed the defendant didn't commit the crime. The jury may well concur that the defendant did have sexual contact with the complainant without her consent. However, when confronted with testimony suggesting that the victim regularly had consensual sex with strangers, the jury might acquit the defendant because they felt that such behavior with that particular woman should not be punished. Obviously, many other factors in the case (such as physical injuries in the victim) may soften the impact of the prior sexual history and produce a different outcome.

From a victim advocate perspective, the strongest formulation of a rape evidence statute would preclude the admission of evidence about the victim's prior sexual conduct with the defendant or with third parties to prove consent, to prove propensity to consent, to prove mistaken belief in consent, to impugn the credibility of the complaining witness, or for any other purpose. It would also restrict the form of evidence offered by barring opinion evidence, specific conduct evidence, reputation evidence, or such evidence in any other form. Lastly, all evidence of the victim's prior sexual history, offered for any purpose, should pass the scrutiny of a *voir dire* hearing, away from the jury and public, to prove relevance. No state has reformed its statutes to this degree.

Most states have confronted the issue by enacting procedural obstacles to the admission of evidence of the complainant's prior sexual history with third parties.[139] A common approach has been to create the statutory presumption prior sexual history is irrelevant to prove consent. The burden of proof, therefore, shifts to the defense in order to show relevance. Some states have provided that the offer of such proof of relevance shall be made in-camera (to the judge in chambers and away from the jury) before any testimony on prior sexual conduct can be heard in open court. Few states have limited cross-examination or restrict the use of sexual history information for the purpose of impeaching credibility; these decisions are generally left to the discretion of the trial court. California is one of the exceptions, having enacted a special evidentiary rule (California Evidence Code, Section 782) that prohibits the introduction of evidence of sexual conduct of the complaining witness to attack credibility. This evidence may be offered, however, if the defense can prove relevance during an in-camera hearing.

Even under the strictist rape shield statutes, the victim's prior sexual history may be admissible under certain circumstances. Few limitations have been placed on testimony relating to the complainant's prior sexual conduct with the defendant. In order to rationally untangle the events on the charged occasion it is important to understand the sexual relationship between the two parties. Prior sexual conduct testimony is usually admissible if used for a so called "noncharacter" purpose. Evidence offered on a noncharacter theory must go neither to credibility nor to conduct (that is, consent); it may be allowed to prove some relevant fact in question. For example, the defense might seek to use prior sexual history information to show modus operandi of prior false charges of rape. Modus operandi evidence differs from character evidence in that it is phrased in descriptively neutral terms (rather than in the rhetoric of moral judgment). Additionally, it must refer to a specific and closely repetitive behavior that is theoretically a more reliable predictor of subsequent conduct than mere evidence of character in general. In many circumstances, the line between permissible modus operandi evidence and impermissible character evidence may be indistinct. The court's discretionary power must come to bear on the decision of admissibility based on the specific arguments presented.

A significant problem faced by the drafters of any rape shield statute is the balancing of the victim's privacy rights against the defendant's right to a fair trial. The Fifth Amendment to the Constitution guarantees a fair trial and due process of law; the Sixth Amendment grants the defendant the right to confront all complaining witnesses against him. The legal literature has been particularly critical of rape shield statutes, arguing that these provisions impinge on constitutional rights that permit any relevant and potentially exculpatory evidence to be heard. The pretrial hearing on relevancy mandated by most reform evidence statutes would seem to obviate these objections.

One aspect of rape shield legislation that is particularly susceptible to constitutional challenge is statutory limitations on cross-examination. American jurisprudence is especially reverent toward cross-examination and regards it as a fundamental building block in the constitutional right of due process.

Another potentially troublesome aspect of rape shield statutes in general is that they address a model system that presumes disposition by trial. As previously discussed, most sexual assault cases are not concluded in the courtroom. Rules of evidence may have an effect on plea bargaining, but only if they significantly influence the bargaining position of one side.[139] Because impirical case data are lacking, the overall effect of rape evidence legislation on plea bargaining outcomes is speculative. Because most reform statutes allow the admission of prior sexual history evidence upon motion, it can be argued that the defense retains (at least theoretically) this bargaining chip. Realistically, rape shield statutes probably favor the prosecution by reducing the likelihood of admitting prior sexual conduct evidence and thus rendering the case less defensible.

The essence of the controversy surrounding rape shield statutes usually centers around the question of whether the probative value of sexual conduct evidence outweighs its prejudicial potential. Obviously, any adverse evidence may, in a sense, be prejudicial to the arguments of one side or the other. In the specific context of sexual assault, however, the important issue is whether the victim's sexual history is necessary and relevant to prove a fact in controversy.

Reformers contend that any other use (especially when introduced to imply that the victim has "bad character") unfairly and inappropriately evokes emotional and irrational responses from the jury, thanks to the widespread and tenacious prejudices against rape victims. At trial, the actual degree of protection from these prejudices may fall short of the legislative intent of rape evidence statutes. One reason is the practical vagueness of the dividing line between probate and prejudice. Another reason is that a number of statutes may bar the prior sexual history for one purpose (consent) but allow it if presented under another theory (credibility). If the jury is going to form an irrational opinion about the complainant based on her prior sexual experiences, the mode of introduction of that information is irrelevant to this prejudicial consequence. Thus, the effectiveness of any rape shield statute depends upon how rigorously probative uses are specified and prejudicial applications are excluded.

Corroboration

Another facet of the jurisprudence of sexual assault that merits discussion is the corroboration requirement.[144] Corroboration in this context refers to statutes in some jurisdictions that require the testimony of the complaining witness to be supported by additional independent evidence to sustain a conviction. In these same jurisdictions the word of the victim of assault, robbery, or other violent crime may alone be sufficient to proceed with prosecution. Justification for treating rape as a unique offense requiring special rules of corroboration is founded on the familiar, but fallacious, argument that men need protection from the false accusations so frequently lodged by malicious and spiteful women. The rebuttals will also be familiar. No empirical evidence or study supports the notion that rape victims lodge false complaints with any greater frequency than do victims of other crimes.[139, 144] It seems illogical to suggest that a woman would voluntarily and unnecessarily subject herself to the disruption, humiliation, and psychosocial trauma usually encountered by the sexual assault victim. In addition, the traditional safeguards of the criminal investigation process and the standard rules of the court are considered sufficient to protect the innocent in every other area of criminal law.

The corroboration issue was one of the first targets of reform. By the early 1970s only fifteen states still had some form of corroboration requirement in sexual assault cases. The product of a strong corroboration statute is a very small number of convictions. As an example, in 1969 in New York City, 1,085 arrests for suspected sexual assault were made. At that time New York state had a very stringent law that required independent corroboration for each material element in the crime—force, penetration, and identity of the accused. The result was a mere eighteen convictions.[144] Most states with similar corroboration statutes (including New York) eventually yielded to pressure from feminists and prosecutors to eliminate or greatly restrict corroboration in rape cases.

Conclusion

After centuries of myth and misconception, society is finally beginning to recognize that all forms of nonconsensual sexual behavior are essentially the same in terms of their potential for physical and psychological harm. As societal norms and attitudes evolve, the law slowly responds to reflect these changes. New laws seldom change attitudes, but new attitudes often change laws. No longer is rape restricted to a single act committed by one sex. Sexual assault, conceptually and legislatively, is now perceived as any form of sexual imposition perpetrated by one individual upon another. Reform efforts during the last fifteen years, spearheaded by the feminist movement, have been substantive and commendable. Certainly all reform objectives have not yet been achieved, but throughout the criminal justice system progressive change continues.

3
The Assailant

I t is helpful for all professionals who must interact with the sexual assault victim to be familiar with the basic needs, motivations, and psychodynamics of the assailant. A realistic understanding of the attacker facilitates empathy by providing a better appreciation of what the victim has been through. Various patterns of rapist behavior produce different constellations of physical trauma and emotional unrest in the victim. The specific features of the assault and the characteristics of the assailant have bearing on a number of important variables. The victim's decision about reporting the crime, the likelihood of arraignment, the probability of conviction, the victim's acute emotional response, and her eventual long-term recovery all vary depending on the details of the rape.[37] The medical examiner who is knowledgeable about the patterns of rape and sensitive to the various victim responses is in an advantageous position to render optimum medical care and appropriate psychological support as well as being a more effective forensic investigator and expert witness.

A major handicap to studying the rapist and his motives has been limited access to offender populations. As previously discussed, most sexual assaults probably go unreported, with as few as 10 percent coming to the attention of authorities. Subtract from the number of reported rapes those in which no arrest is made and from the arrest group subtract those cases in which conviction is not obtained. The final product is a relatively small group of convicted sexual offenders that accounts for only a fraction of the "rapist" population in general. Unfortunately, rapists seldom present voluntarily to the mental health system in search of help.[172] Information about sexual offenders, therefore, comes almost exclusively from studying convicted assailants. Because no data exist about the much larger group of undetected rapists, it is somewhat speculative to make inferences about the total group based on information obtained from the smaller convicted group.[37, 38]

The same superstructure of myth and misconception that surrounds the sexual assault victim influences the public's perception of the rapist. Popular stereotypes include the lustful man who falls prey to a provocative and vindictive woman, the amorous but frustrated soul who succumbs to the pressure of his pent-up needs, and the psychotic and perverted sex fiend who attempts to quell his insatiable desires. The common denominator here is the assumption that rape is primarily motivated by sexual desire.

Based on work with convicted felons, Groth and Birnbaum have concluded that to portray the rapist as oversexed is oversimplistic and inaccurate.[172] The presumption that rape occurs as a result of sexual frustration without outlet was not substantiated by their population. Most of their offenders (whether married or not) were, at the time of the assault, sexually active in consenting relationships. To continue to regard rape as an expression of sexual passion is not only invalid but also carries the liability of shifting the focus of responsibility from assailant behavior to victim conduct. Groth and Birnbaum further assert that rape is always a symptom of some underlying psychological dysfunction. Generally, the individual who rapes is ill-equipped to manage the stresses and frustrations of daily life. He is emotionally weak and insecure but not psychotic or retarded. He is generally unable to establish or maintain any close or intimate relationships with other people; he lacks the capacity for warmth, sharing, trust, or empathy. As stress mounts and inner emotional turmoil increases, his judgment deteriorates. Without regard for the consequences, the rapist resorts to the desperate act of sexual assault as his method of discharging the anxiety that he perceives will otherwise destroy him. Sex for the rapist, therefore, is a vehicle for acting out; it may be a compensatory tool or a retaliatory weapon. Sexual gratification is not his objective per se, but rather the means for attenuating a painful inner state of dysphoria.

With the potential for sampling bias in mind, Groth, Burgess, and Holmstrom attempted to conceptualize a clinical typology of rape using an analysis of experiential accounts of rape from convicted offenders and rape victims.[38] The offender group was derived from a random sample of 133 convicted rapists committed for clinical assessment to the Massachusetts Center for Diagnosis and Treatment of Sexually Dangerous Persons. The victim group included ninety-two adult women who were part of a one-year counseling and research study conducted at Boston City Hospital. The 225 total offenses were congruent in time, but there were no victim-offender matches.

Certainly no two assaults are the same nor are any two assailants identical, but some interesting patterns emerged from this study. (See table 3–1.) In every one of the 225 offenses analyzed, three elements were present: power, anger, and sexuality. The relative intensity of each varied from case to case as did specific modes of expression, but in each assault all three components were present to some degree. Either power or anger was predominant in each rape with sexuality consistently taking a role subservient to the primary motivating factor. Rape is a pseudosexual act with sexuality merely the vehicle for expression of either power or anger; rape is not primarily an expression of sexual desire, but rather sexual behavior in the service of nonsexual needs.

In a "power rape" the assailant uses threats, a weapon or physical force to render the victim helpless and submissive to his

Table 3–1
Differences between Power and Anger Rapes

Characteristic	Power Rape	Anger Rape
Premeditation	Common	Unusual
Victim age group	Same as assailant	May be older or elderly
Principal motivation	Coitus as proof of conquest	Vent rage at women
Force used	Sufficient to insure compliance	Far more than required to gain submission

total control. The aim of this type of assault is the achievement of sexual intercourse as evidence of conquest, not sexual gratification. The power rapist often suffers from low self-esteem and inadequate interpersonal skills; sexuality may be the foundation of his self-image and rape becomes an important method for affirming his strength, potency, and identity. Power rapes are premeditated and often preceded by obsessional fantasies in which the victim initially resists, but once subdued, submits responsively and gratefully to the offender's masterful sexual technique. The victim's response never matches the fantasy and the offender is left disappointed, unsatisfied, and frustrated; he will probably rape again as the search for the perfect experience continues.

Sexual dysfunction in the form of erective inadequacy, premature or retarded ejaculation, may complicate the power rapist's problems and limit the physical evidence available for collection at the evidentiary exam. There is usually no conscious intent from this type of offender to hurt or degrade his victim. The use of threats or force is generally only that which is required to insure submission to the assailant's control. Consequently, many victims of power rapists will show signs of minimal, nonspecific trauma (small extragenital scratches, abrasions, eccymoses, etc.) or no signs of trauma at all. The dearth of objective physical evidence in this type of assault in no way minimizes the effect of the event on the victim and the medical examiner must respond accordingly.

The "anger rape" is a brutal assault to all parts of the body in which the offender expresses anger, rage, contempt, and hatred for his victim. Far more force than necessary is used to subdue his victim and the victim is often forced to submit to a variety of degrading physical and verbal abuses. A significant portion of the injuries may occur after the sexual part of the assault has been completed. The aim of this type of rape is to vent rage against the victim in retaliation for perceived wrongs or rejections the assailant has suffered at the hands of women. The offender may subconsciously find sex disgusting and derives little or no sexual satisfaction from the assault; sexuality is a weapon he uses to brutalize his victim. His history is often full of unsuccessful relationships with women, punctuated with conflict, irrationality, and violence. His sexual assaults may be sporadic and spontaneous, often triggered by conflicts with significant women in his life (mother, wife) with his rage displaced to the victim. The offender experiences the rape with conscious anger and sadistic excitement; he intends to hurt, punish, and degrade his victim. He experiences satisfaction and relief not so much from sexual gratification as from vented rage.

As with power rapists, anger rapists may suffer from erective inadequacy and retarded ejaculation, but the examination of their victims is usually quite different. Power rapists usually select victims about their own age, while older women may be the targets of anger rapists. Anger rape victims are often severely injured with both genital and nongenital trauma and "perverted acts" are frequently a main component of the assault. These victims may have life-threatening injuries requiring surgery and/or hospitalization.

The extreme form of anger rape is termed sadistic rape.[172] In this pattern aggression and sexuality merge into the psychological experience of sadism. Brutality becomes eroticized as the assailant derives excitement and gratification from his deliberate sexual and physical abuse of the victim. Sadistic rape frequently involves bondage, torture, degrading acts, foreign objects, or ritualistic behavior. Victims may be symbolic in the sense that they share some common trait or characteristic (such as prostitutes or adolescents). This type of rapist may experience sexual arousal in proportion to the victim's pain and degree of resistance. The majority of rape-homicides probably fall into this category.

In their detailed study of 225 rapes, Groth, Burgess, and Holmstrom found the majority (64.5 percent) to be power rapes. The remaining 35.5 percent were classified as anger rapes, but sixty-one of the seventy-nine total offenses in the anger group came from the offender sample of the study population. The violent nature of the anger rape probably contributes to a higher conviction rate and, thus, may have spuriously raised the overall percentage of anger rapes in this study.

The relatively new discipline of forensic psychology is helping dispel some of the longstanding myths about the rapist and his psychopathology. The offender should be viewed as a deeply troubled individual who acts out sexually in response to stresses in his environment; his behavior is not the consequence of unmet sexual desire. Rape is not aggressive sexuality but rather sexuality in the service of aggression. All who must deal with the rape victim will do so more effectively and humanely when equipped with a more accurate and rational understanding of the offense and the offender.

4
Medical History, Examination, and Evidence Collection

T he person responsible for performing the evidential examination on the adult sexual assault survivor has been quite
variable. Historically, it was not uncommon for this activity to fall
within the province of the county medical examiner or police
surgeon. If such civil resources were unavailable, the "on call"
gynecologist for the local public hospital usually acquired the task.
Some communities were able to muster a panel of private physicians
(usually gynecologists) who would rotate the responsibility for
doing the exams. The increasing number of exams (with most
occurring in the middle of the night) and the often low reimburse-
ment, coupled with the anxiety and disruption associated with
testimony in court, have traditionally been potent deterrents to
voluntary physician participation.

The justification for requiring physician involvement is multifaceted.[191] The physician-patient relationship is often reverently
cited as the optimum facilitator of trust, veracity, and reassurance.
Physicians are expected to possess both the expertise and societal
approval for evaluating female genitalia. A commonly held belief in
the legal community is that physicians are more credible witnesses
than other health care providers. The necessity of twenty-four-hour
coverage and the potential need to treat rape-related injuries and risks
(pregnancy and sexually transmitted diseases) have created a trend
toward incorporating sexual assault exams into the regular duties of
the emergency room physician. Most exams today are conducted in
the emergency department by a staff physician.

Despite the compelling nature of these arguments, the prevailing system has some significant flaws. A successful sexual assault exam must incorporate not only sound medical treatment but also meticulous evidence collection technique and a special sensitivity to the psychosocial needs of the victim. The key to putting all the pieces together is adequate training. Unfortunately, few emergency department physicians have had sufficient preparation in the theory and conduct of the evidential exam. This deficiency is often further compromised by the pervasive misconceptions about rape to which unenlightened physicians are just as susceptible as the general population.

The emergency room may be a convenient resource for unscheduled medical needs but is far from the ideal setting for the evidential exam. The atmosphere is frequently frenetic and stressful, which may intensify the emotional turmoil and anxiety that the victim is experiencing. Most emergency departments are organized with single-physician coverage. From the rape victim's perspective, the results are long delays (often hours) before the exam begins and frequent interruptions as the physician is called away to attend to more urgent or life-threatening medical problems.

The outcome of this process may produce a scenario with more negative features than positive. The harried emergency physician may be ill-equipped for this unique medical-legal encounter and approach the victim with skepticism and animosity. The examiner's unfamiliarity with the compulsory details of evidence collection and the long delays inherent in the system can severely hamper the criminalist's ability to contribute forensic corroboration. The district attorney may have to prepare the case from a suboptimal medical report and then be faced with a reluctant and undertrained medical "expert." The victim has the most to lose. She probably has just been through the most terrifying and traumatic experience of her life. What she requires is a calm environment and the support of sympathetic and knowledgeable professionals; what she often gets is a surrealistic misadventure populated with people who don't fully understand her needs or the nature of her trauma.

The Sexual Assault Exam Team

A number of communities have advanced some innovative alternatives to the traditional emergency department approach.[191, 192, 193] Some hospitals afford priority status to rape victims and curtail the usual admissions red tape; they may provide a special entrance or even a separate and secluded area of the hospital in which to conduct the interview and exam. In some locales the exam may be performed in a public health facility, a mental health facility, or perhaps a rape crisis center. In sites away from a hospital, emergency medical treatment may be rendered elsewhere before the exam or, if injuries are minor, after the exam has been completed.

The most intriguing new concept in sexual assault evaluation is the use of specially trained nursing personnel or physician assistants to perform the entire exam.[191, 192, 193] This approach offers promise in alleviating many of the problems inherent in the traditional physician/emergency room exam system. The first advantage is that midlevel practitioners can be selected as examiners based on their sincere desire to help the victim and on their interest in conducting the evidential encounter. This motivation and altruism is an excellent foundation for a comprehensive training program addressing all aspects (medical, legal, psychosocial) of the rape experience and sexual assault evaluation. Sensitivity, positive attitude, and special education are functionally much more important attributes than professional title.

The use of nonphysician sexual assault examiners is consistent with a larger, more general trend in health care over the last decade, which has seen the development of nursing subspecialization (stomal care, hospice services, diabetic education, and so on) and midlevel practitioners (physician assistants and nurse practitioners.) A central benefit of these extended roles has been the opportunity to develop genuine expertise in a specific clinical area. Experience from pilot programs in which nurses perform evidential exams has been very encouraging.[191, 192] In Florida, for example, not only has victim response been favorable but also the integrity of collected evidence has been excellent.[191] Feedback from the criminal justice system (judges, prosecutors, juries) in this Florida community has also been extremely positive and has found the nurse examiners to have the same credibility as physicians when called to testify.[191] This is also supported by the fact that no decrease in conviction rates has occurred since nurses have become responsible for the rape exams.[193]

Improved efficiency and more timely evidence collection are additional advantages of a nurse-examiner–based program. Most pilot projects have structured an on-call system facilitating prompt response when a sexual assault victim presents for evaluation and care.[191, 192] Because the examiner's only responsibility is to the victim, she need not compete with other patients for provider time. Emergency department nursing and social service resources may also be spared for other duties because the specially trained nurse examiner can generally be expected to function independently and attend to the spectrum of victim needs. The cost effectiveness of a system based on nursing time rather than physician time has obvious appeal for both the prosecutor and the hospital administrator.

As favorable reports continue to emerge in support of nonphysician sexual assault examiners, more communities may well consider implementing such a program. But because interest, needs and resources vary from setting to setting it is unlikely that every locale will be able to develop its own "ideal" system. Two points here deserve emphasis. First, centralization of resources for evaluation and management of rape victims may lack convenience from the standpoint of travel time but more than compensates from the enhanced quality of victim support and evidence collection that volume and experience provide. In many areas this process already operates defacto because most hospitals in a given community may refuse to do the exams, often shunting victims to the local county hospital or its functional equivalent. As stressed earlier, comprehensive training is always important for any health care provider who interacts with sexual assault victims but it should be considered absolutely essential in those hospitals responsible for providing care for the area's rape victims.

The second point that needs to be stressed is the importance of teamwork, cooperation, effective communication, and flexibility as necessary ingredients to optimize functioning in any sexual assault program. In many situations it may be possible to significantly improve services to rape victims simply by adjusting existing resources rather than creating new ones. For example, it might be helpful in some settings for the emergency room nurse (with appropriate training) to assume a greater role by taking the victim's history and performing the nongenital evidence collection. The physician could then briefly review the history and perform the genital exam and specimen collection. Another example could be the use of rape crisis volunteers to provide support by accompanying the victim during the evaluation and educating her about the trauma of rape and the details of the medical-legal encounter. In communities where nurses or midlevel practitioners conduct the examination (especially those in nonhospital settings) a close working relationship with the physician back-up is mandatory for the evaluation and management of significant injuries and rape-related risks (sexually transmitted disease and pregnancy).

Reporting Requirements and Consent Issues

The responsibility for reporting sexual crimes to law enforcement is extremely variable. Who is required to report (physician, nurse, social worker, etc.), as well as which specific crimes mandate notification of authorites, varies from jurisdiction to jurisdiction. In general, state statutes usually provide guidelines, but in many instances the practical application of the law is left to the discretion of the local district attorney and police authorities. Because failure to comply with statutory notification procedures frequently engenders criminal penalties, it behooves any health professional who may interact with sexual assault victims to be familiar both with state law and the prevailing local interpretations of the reporting requirements.

Because the examination of the rape victim generates potential evidence that must stand up in court, adherence to the rules governing written, witnessed, informed consent is essential. Failure to comply not only jeopardizes acceptance of the collected information and material as evidence but may also place the medical examiner in a precarious position from a liability standpoint.[15] Each phase of the medical and evidential exam requires specific consent.[9, 16, 17, 19] Consent for evaluation and treatment of medical problems is the same as for any other patient who presents to the emergency department in need of care. Additional, separate consents must be obtained for any photos that are taken, for the collection and performance of special forensic tests, for the release of any physical evidence from the hospital laboratory to the criminalistics laboratory, and finally for the release of information from the patient's hospital record to appropriate authorities in the criminal justice system. Medical and evidentiary evaluation of minors is more complex but generally requires the signature of a parent or legal guardian.[9, 15, 16, 19]

An important but sometimes misunderstood area involves the victim's right to consent for medical treatment (including evaluation of both physical and emotional trauma, detection and/or prevention of venereal disease or prevention of pregnancy) and refuse consent for the evidential exam. Even if the patient plans not to pursue legal action at the time of the exam she should be strongly encouraged to undergo the evidential portion of the exam. Time is of the essence in collection of specimens and evaluation of any physical evidence that might help corroborate her testimony or identify the perpetrator should she change her mind at a later time.[9, 17]

Obtaining the History

Even before the structured portion of the evidential exam begins, every effort should be made to help assuage the victim's anxiety and feelings of vulnerability. The importance of providing tranquil surroundings and minimizing registration paperwork has already been mentioned. The rape victim should not be left alone as that may well intensify her emotional upset. The trained rape crisis worker, as discussed earlier, is an excellent resource who can support the victim and answer her questions while waiting for the exam to commence.

The effect of the examiner's attitude and demeanor on the victim cannot be underestimated. Most victims are already struggling with significant feelings of guilt and self-recrimination, and quickly perceive even subtle cues from the clinician that may suggest suspicion or disbelief. The result can be increased emotional trauma and prolonged recovery. Despite gut feelings, the safest and most humane tack is to automatically assume a rape has occurred and conduct the encounter accordingly. It is certainly preferable to err on the side of sympathy and support. A few minutes spent at the outset establishing rapport and conveying empathy not only make the subsequent history and exam go more smoothly but also pay long-term dividends in helping the victim deal successfully with the traumatic event she has endured.

The objectives of the history fall into two categories. The first is to identify and delineate specific historical information and any acute complaints that may require medical investigation and/or treatment. Evaluation and therapy of acute injuries in the rape victim should proceed as they do for any other patient. Historical data regarding allergies, current medication, and tetanus immunization status are of obvious importance to insure the patient receives optimum medical care. Treatment concerns unique to the rape victim, such as potential venereal disease or pregnancy, deserve special attention and are discussed in more detail subsequently.

The second objective of the history is to guide the medical-legal examination to specific areas that may yield corroborating physical evidence. It is very important that the history be only detailed enough to focus the examiner's efforts on the areas of potential findings. Too many details in the medical history may actually jeopardize the victim's chances for a conviction.[7, 9, 12, 18, 19] Regardless of external demeanor, the victim is upset and distraught; information given under these circumstances may be confusing. Months later, at the time of the trial, minor discrepancies between the medical history and the police report may emerge, which impugn the victim's credibility and destroy the prosecution's case. Most authorities prefer a "check-off" or "fill in the blanks" history form that is thorough and complete but at the same time not tediously detailed. Information on this form should be sufficient to smoothly direct the examination and easily refresh the examiner's memory before testimony.

The history from the rape victim (see figure 4–1) includes standard medical data and a number of specific questions regarding the details of the assault. The history should begin with some basic

Demographic Information
    Age
    Race
    Interpreter (if used)

Past Medical History
    Current actue or chronic illness
    Medications
    Allergies
    Tetanus immunization status
    Preattack injuries
        (age/description)
    If appropriate—
        Major psychiatric illness/
            treatment
        Drug/alcohol use near the time of
            the assault

Gynecologic History
    Last menstrual period
        (regularity of cycles)
    Consensual intercourse within
        seventy-two hours prior to
        assault (if yes, when?)
    Recent gynecologic injury, surgery,
        procedure, infection, or treatment
        that may influence current physi-
        cal findings

Assault History
    Specific physical complaints/injuries
    Date/time of assault
    Location and description of assault
        surroundings
    Assailant: Number (who did what?)
        Race
        If appropriate: relationship to victim
    Methods employed by assailant:
        Weapon (type, injuries inflicted)
        Use of physical restraints
        Use of threats
        Nature of physical contact/ struggle
            (blows, grasping, bites, choking,
            etc.)
    Description of sexual acts
        Penetration of vagina and/or rectum
        Oral copulation of genitals and/or
            anus
        Masturbation
        Fondling, licking, kissing, biting
        Foreign object use (what? where?)
        Use of foam, jelly, lubricant, saliva
        Use of condom by assailant
        Ejaculation on body surface
        Degrading acts (describe)
    Postassault cleanup activities
        Bathing
        Douching
        Wiping (describe)
        Tampon/sponge/diaphram re-
            moved or inserted
        Teeth brushing or gargling
        Bowel movement
        Clothing change

Figure 4–1. *Important Elements in the Victim's History of Sexual
Assault*

demographic information. Documenting the patient's age is not only a basic part of the medical history but also has legal ramifications concerning the consent issue. The ethnicity of the victim (and the assailant, if known) is important to record because this information may be essential in the interpretation of some forensic tests. If the history is obtained with the aid of an interpreter, that person should be clearly identified and documented.

Past medical history should include a discussion of any current acute or chronic medical problems that could influence the interpretation of the physical findings or bear on treatment considerations. Correlative to this is the description and age of any preassault injuries so there will be no confusion in the interpretation of attack-related findings. Because medical expert testimony often focuses on the significance of minor injuries, it is prudent to thoroughly describe any findings, however subtle or seemingly inconsequential.

Some past medical history items may be important in assessing the victim's ability to grant lawful consent but may also be used as a lever by the defense to impugn her credibility. One such issue is major psychiatric illness and treatment. If the victim seems significantly impaired at the time of the exam the most practical approach is a psychiatric consultation to help ascertain her competence. Another problematic area is the use of alcohol and/or drugs before or after the assault. Intoxication may be to a degree that it invalidates consent but may also be used to attack credibility or to imply that the encounter was consensual. Some protocols require blood alcohol levels and/or toxicology screens routinely, but most advocate their use only if the index of suspicion is high. If the prevailing local standard calls for these tests or if the victim seems to be under the influence of something and the clinician requests they be collected, it is appropriate to obtain pertinent historical data to help interpret the results. Being straightforward with the victim about what is being collected and why tends to improve the accuracy of the history.

Probably the most controversial part of the medical inquiry revolves around the victim's gynecologic history. The focal legal point here is the defense attorney's access to the victim's prior sexual history. Information about gravidity, parity, abortions, miscarriages, and contraception may be standard questions in the medical evaluation of a gynecologic problem but can severely disadvantage the victim in court without serving any constructive purpose in the evidential examination.

As a general principle, only information essential to the interpretation of physical findings or laboratory data should be recorded. These items include last menstrual period, because the time in the menstrual cycle may influence some forensic data such as sperm motility and recovery. Current menses may be a nontraumatic source of blood found in the vagina. From a treatment perspective, the last menstrual period (including a notation about the regularity of cycling) has obvious implications to assess pregnancy risk or the possibility of preexisting pregnancy, which could preclude the use of some medications for STD prophylaxis. Another appropriate item to record is any recent gynecologic surgery, procedure, infection, or treatment relevant to the analysis of the physical findings.

If the victim professes to have been virginal before the assault, information about tampon use is helpful. If the victim has had recent consensual intercourse, semen from her partner could potentially complicate the forensic evaluation of assault-related material. Some protocols ask for the date and time of the last consensual intercourse (LCI). This information may be an unnecessary intrusion into the victim's personal life. Since the critical period for semen analysis is the first seventy-two hours after ejaculation, it is best to ask the victim if she has had intercourse within the three-day period before the assault. If the response is affirmative, it is appropriate to request the date and time of the coitus. Whether the consensual partner wore a condom or has undergone vasectomy should also be documented.

A number of items must be included in the description of the assault and the postassault period. The date and time of the assault are obviously important for medical, legal, and forensic reasons. The date and time of the first report of the assault and the time of the exam must be recorded. A number of important decisions and interpretations are based on the time interval between assault and exam. Any unusual delay between the time of the assault and the time of report should be explained. The location of the assault and a description of the specific surroundings may provide subtle but essential corroboration. For example, a rape at the beach should yield some sand; an assault in a field should leave some grass or debris that can be collected. If physical restraints were used, they should be described and the examiner's attention focused to look for the typical linear abrasions or erythema.

The nature of the struggle (if any) should be documented and an appropriate search made for the frequently found evidence of minor trauma (eccymoses, abrasions, erythema). If there was no struggle, why not? Was a weapon alleged or seen? If threats of violence or reprisal were used to subjugate the victim and prevent resistance, this should be noted. Correlative to the victim's account of the struggle is her description of how her clothing was removed and if any damage was done. The record should indicate whether she was wearing the same clothing at the time of the examination.

A detailed description of the assailant(s) is a law enforcement responsibility and not appropriate for the medical report. Some information about the attacker, however, is relevant in the sexual assault evaluation. The number of assailants and who did what should be clearly noted to allow the criminalist to accurately interpret forensic data from different sites and different individuals. Likewise, the ethnicity of the assailant(s) is necessary since certain genetic markers recovered from evidence material have variable prevalence depending on race. If the victim injured the assailant in any way (especially if she scratched him), this may provide important corroboration after his apprehension and may help focus the criminalist's attention on fingernail scraping evidence. Some protocols request information about the assailant's relationship to the victim (stranger, acquaintance, date, former lover, and so on) and/or his name. This may help corroborate the victim's account of the incident but unless specifically required should be omitted because of prior sexual history concerns.

A thorough characterization of all sexual acts is obviously a central issue in the evidential exam. This information is also extremely sensitive and it is usually quite difficult for the victim (and possibly for the examiner) to discuss. This is especially stressful for younger victims and if rectal or degrading acts occurred. Because this information is so intimate, it is advantageous to leave this part of the encounter until near the end of the history when rapport has had a chance to develop. As a preface to the discussion of sexual acts, it is helpful to acknowledge the embarrassing and painful nature of the inquiry. The victim must understand that accurate and complete information is essential not only to guide the evidence collection but also to ensure that a thorough exam is done to rule out injury. Often the victim will draw solace when she learns that each distinct act engenders a separate charge and corresponding penalty so her candor in describing what happened will be rewarded by appropriate punishment of the perpetrator.

Particularly apropos to the description of sexual acts is a "check off the boxes" format. To complete this line by line with the victim helps ensure accurate and complete data. As a caveat here, make sure the victim understands the question exactly. It may be necessary to use colloquial terminology or slang to promote accuracy. Information covered should include the victim's account of any penetration of rectum or vagina by finger, penis, or foreign object. Details regarding foreign object use is important to focus the examination for potential injury and to alert the police to search the crime scene for the object. Any oral copulation or masturbation must be described. The victim's impression about ejaculation (inside a body orifice or on the surface of the body) is essential to guide the evidence collection. The use of foam, jelly, or lubricant (including saliva) must be recorded since many commercial products and saliva can affect the forensic evaluation of semen and sperm. Fondling, licking, or kissing should be noted and swabs taken because recovered saliva may yield forensic evidence helpful in identifying the assailant. Condom use by the assailant, although unusual, should be recorded because it will affect recovery of seminal products. Lastly in this section, the victim should be given the opportunity to relate anything else (such as degrading acts) that happened to her.

Victims universally feel "dirty" after an assault and any cleanup efforts (washing, wiping, bathing, douching) must be specified because they may influence the results of the forensic evaluation. If the victim wiped her perineum or any semen on her skin immediately after the assault, this should be noted and the wipe described so it can be collected and analyzed. It may contain significant and relatively uncontaminated seminal evidence. In the case of fellatio or sodomy, evidence may be lost if the victim brushed her teeth, gargled, vomited, or moved her bowels. If the victim was wearing a tampon, diaphragm, or contraceptive sponge during the assault, this should be noted. If it is still in place at the time of the genital exam, it should be removed, thoroughly dried in a stream of cool air and saved for forensic analysis. If the victim removed it after the assault, law enforcement should be alerted so that it may be retrieved for the crime lab.

Physical Examination and Evidence Collection

The physical examination of the adult female victim of sexual assault has two main focuses: medical and legal (see figure 4–2). The primary goal is recognition, evaluation, and treatment of any injuries or complaints. Obviously, expedient attention to physical trauma, especially if it is serious or life threatening, takes the highest priority of the clinician's time and expertise. This aspect of the encounter does not differ from that of any other emergency department patient. The other important medical aspect of the encounter is prophylaxis against the development of sexually transmitted disease or unwanted pregnancy as a result of the assault.

The second focus of the examination, the legal portion, is quite unique in the practice of clinical medicine. The goal here is the collection, preservation, and, to some degree, interpretation of

Medical
   Evaluate and treat injuries or complaints (physical and emotional)
   Prophylax against potential sexually transmitted disease and/or pregnancy
      consequent to sexual assault

Legal
   Substantiate the victim's ability or inability to have granted lawful consent
   Document any objective findings of recent trauma
   Document any physical signs consistent with a recent sexual act
   Collect and preserve appropriate physical evidence for further forensic
      evaluation

Figure 4–2. *Objectives for the Evidential Examination of the Sexual Assault Victim*

evidence that may corroborate the alleged offense. A number of legal questions must be addressed and determinations made based on the findings of the medical examiner and the subsequent evaluation by the criminalistics laboratory of physical evidence collected at the time of the examination. The victim's ability to have given lawful consent at the time of the assault is also very important. Objective evidence of trauma may substantiate the use of force and the victim's resistance to it. The physical findings consistent with penetration and/or the occurrence of a recent sexual act are critical to the preparation of the prosecution's case. Lastly, the collection of evidence from the victim may provide information helpful in corroborating the history or establishing the positive identification of the perpetrator after he is apprehended.

As previously discussed, many examiners who are requested to perform evidentiary examinations on rape victims may find themselves in an unfamiliar and uncomfortable arena because they lack experience or special training in the procedure and conduct of the medical-legal examination. Several points relative to the unique nature of this type of exam deserve emphasis. The first point involves "preservation of the chain of evidence."[2, 7, 9, 16] This refers to the custody of evidence as it changes hands at each step from collection, to transport, to evaluation, to presentation in court. Each person who handles the evidence must be sequentially and accurately recorded. If the chain is broken or anything is improperly labeled, that piece of evidence is effectively invalidated and not usable in court. A second point is the importance of a disciplined, methodical collection of evidence. The examination and search for evidence should be carefully guided by the history in the context of the specific protocol set up by local authorities. Strict adherence to jurisdictional variations in the criminal justice system and methodological idiosyncrasies of the specific criminalistics laboratory is essential to ensure integrity of the results. Local guidelines from both the district attorney's office and the crime lab must be developed and strictly followed.

The examination (see figure 4–3) logically commences with an assessment of the patient's demeanor and mental status. After taking the history and, thus, interacting with the patient for a few minutes, the clinician should have a reasonable idea about whether

Physical Examination
    Document date and time of exam and specimen collection
    Assess demeanor and mental status
    General physical exam with specific focus on complaints or injuries
    Dermal examination with documentation of any signs of recent trauma or
        foreign material and/or stains
    Mouth exam—signs of trauma; GC culture if indicated
    Pelvic exam
        Vulva—erythema, edema, signs of trauma
            Introitus/hymen—description, elasticity, signs of trauma
        Vagina—signs of trauma
        Cervix—signs of trauma, GC culture, (chlamydia culture)
        Bimanual—tenderness, signs of infection or pregnancy
        Rectal (if indicated)—signs of trauma, GC culture

Evidence Collection
    Assault clothing and debris
    Wood's lamp examination—collection of suspicious material or stains and
        reference swabs from similar area without stains
    Reference head hairs
    Reference pubic hairs
    Pubic combings
    Fingernail scrapings
    Saliva sample for secretor status
    Vaginal pool sampling—motile sperm evaluation, swabs for forensic evaluation
    Blood—VDRL, ABO blood typing, (blood alcohol/toxicology, if indicated)
    Oral/rectal sampling (if indicated)
    Pregnancy testing (if indicated)
    Toxicology screening (if indicated)
    Urine toxicology

Figure 4–3. *Evidential Examination of the Sexual Assault Victim*

there has been consumption of alcohol and/or drugs to a significant enough degree to effect lawful consent. Verification by toxicological assessment is prudent. As mentioned above, the suspicion of a major psychiatric problem, thought disorder, or mental retardation should prompt a formal mental status exam or psychiatric consultation because these issues are germane to lawful consent. A variety of reaction patterns have been described in the immediate postassault period and will be discussed in more detail later. Acknowledgment and description of the victim's emotional state are important for preparation of the district attorney's case as well as for potential treatment/referral.

    Variation from setting to setting is common, but it is often the responsibility of the medical examiner or nurse to describe and briefly examine the victim's clothing. The report should mention whether the clothes currently worn are the same that were worn during the assault and any damage to the clothing or stains should be documented. No attempt should be made to remove any stain or foreign material; this must be done under controlled conditions in the criminalistics lab.

A member of the evidentiary examination team, preferably female, should watch the patient (who should be barefoot) remove the "assault" clothing over two clean sheets or two pieces of clean exam table paper so as to catch any foreign material that might be potentially significant evidence. The top sheet is folded to capture any trace evidence and placed in the clothing bag. The second sheet prevents contamination from the floor and is discarded. The clothing and folded sheet should then be placed into a paper bag (not plastic, because it can promote mold growth on seminal stains) and given to the officer after appropriate labeling and attention to "chain of evidence" details. It is important that the clothing not be folded across any obvious stains. No one but the victim should handle the clothing because 70–80 percent of the population are "secretors" and inadvertent contamination with perspiration or body oils may leave traces that could confuse or invalidate the forensic evaluation of the clothing.[15, 79] If exam team members handle the clothing, they should wear gloves. The patient should then be modestly gowned and made ready for the formal physical exam.

A careful head-to-toe inspection of the victim's skin should be undertaken to note any signs of trauma (however minimal) and detection of foreign material that might help corroborate the victim's account. The history is particularly helpful in this phase of the exam and should focus the clinician's attention to specific areas that may yield subtle findings consistent with the victim's description of the assault (see figure 4–4). Common minor injuries may include grip marks (linear, parallel erythematous lines) on the anterior neck or upper arms, small abrasions or eccymoses on the breasts and medial thighs, and tiny eccymoses on the perioral area or anterior gums if the victim's mouth was covered by the assailant's hand.[1, 15, 16] If the victim was bound, there may be linear abrasions

Dermal
  Grip marks (linear, parallel, erythematous lines) on the anterior neck or arms
  Small abrasions or eccymoses on the breasts or medial thighs
  Tiny eccymoses on the perioral region or on the buccal surfaces of the gums
  Linear abrasions or erythema on the wrists or ankles if bound

Perineal
  Clitoral and/or labial enlargement (1–2 hours)
  Posterior fourchette erythema (several hours)
  Microtrauma of the introitus, vagina, or cervix (as visualized by culposcopy or
    after toluidine blue application)

Figure 4–4. *Common Subtle Physical Findings in the Sexual Assault*
Victim

or erythema on the wrists.[15] The back should be carefully inspected for both foreign matter and characteristic impressions or small indentations that could help confirm the location of the assault if the victim was forced to lie supine on a hard or dirty surface.[9] Accurate documentation of any dermal findings is essential. Color photographs or drawings are often used but should be supplemented with a careful written description of each finding.

Bite marks deserve special attention. If the victim is seen shortly after the injury, indentations from the assailant's teeth may still be apparent on the victim's skin. With proper documentation, this may provide what is called a "jigsaw match" with the assailant's teeth if he is apprehended. A few communities have specially trained forensic dentists who, if available on an on-call basis, can make casts of the bite marks and from the suspect's mouth to conclusively include or exclude him as the "biter." In most cases such a resource will not be available, so the next best alternative is a close-up color photograph. The photo must include a scale to give accurate dimension to the injury and should be taken with tangential lighting to bring out the detail in relief. As with any other contact potentially involving the assailant's saliva, any bite (recent or not) should be swabbed and a nearby control swab taken. Labeling and drying of swabs is done in the usual fashion.

A Wood's light inspection of the dermis in general and the perineum in particular may help identify seminal stains by their brilliant fluorescence.[1, 7, 10] It is important to note that moist seminal stains do not fluoresce the same way that dried stains do.

Any suspicious material should be swabbed with a labeled cotton or dacron swab moistened with saline or distilled water, air dried for sixty minutes in a stream of cool air and placed in a labeled evidence envelope. Thick or crusted stains may be scraped directly into a labeled evidence envelope with the edge of a clean glass microscope slide. When *any* stain is collected, the record should clearly indicate where it is from and the location of the complementary "control" swabs taken from an adjacent unstained area. Control swabs should also be clearly labeled.

Fingernail scrapings from the victim should be obtained and placed in another envelope; these samples may contain material from the assailant. Any debris or foreign matter that is collected needs the same compulsive labeling. It is helpful to the criminalist to indicate what the debris seems to be (cloth fiber, grass, dirt, etc.).

The patient is next placed in the dorsal lithotomy position for the perineal portion of the examination. A clean sheet or piece of exam table paper is placed under the victim's buttocks. If not already completed, the perineum is examined with the Wood's light. Any suspicious material is either scraped (if dried on the skin) or removed with a moistened cotton or dacron swab (as previously described). If material is within the pubic hair, it is clipped out in toto and placed in an envelope. The pubic hair is then combed with a clean, fine-tooth comb or fine-bristle brush and both combings and comb (or brush) are placed in an envelope. Foreign matter on hairs from the victim are thus collected.[113] Fifteen to twenty of the victim's pubic hairs and head hair should be plucked or clipped very close to the skin for forensic evaluation. These "reference hairs" should be obtained from random locations to adequately sample variation in victim hair morphology.

The vulva is carefully evaluated for signs of trauma or recent sexual intercourse. Vulvar trauma in the sexually active adult female from intercourse alone is unusual.[1, 16, 19, 35] Most reported vulvar injuries occur in children and elderly victims with the predominant lesions being minor tears of the posterior fourchette between the four o'clock and eight o'clock position, with most at six o'clock.[1, 9, 15, 35] Obviously, if a foreign object or unusual force is used, there may well be corresponding injuries. The examiner should be alert to some of the subtle signs of recent sexual activity (see figure 4–4), which include engorgement of the labia and clitoris and erythema of the posterior fourchette. Engorgement usually fades in one to two hours after coitus, while the erythema may be present for several hours.[16, 25] These signs are somewhat nonspecific because consensual intercourse or manual stimulation may also produce engorgement and/or erythema but their presence should be noted because they may help confirm the history.

Two ancillary methods for improving the detection threshold of microtrauma after intercourse have recently been suggested. The first involves the use of the culposcope, whose magnified, stereoscopic image allows the examiner to closely scrutinize the introitus, vagina, and cervix for tiny mucosal lacerations consequent to coitus.[167] The second method uses the application of toluidine blue dye, a nuclear stain, to introital and vaginal mucosa.[194, 195] Even very small violations of the epidermis, not seen with the naked eye, are highlighted as the exposed dermal nuclei take up the dye.

Both of these modalities are commonly used in the evaluation of children suspected of being sexually abused. In children, who are obviously not sexually active normally, penetration is more likely to cause trauma and any finding consistent with penetration is abnormal. A positive culposcopic exam or any toluidine blue staining helps confirm the offense. Unfortunately, the situation is not so straightforward in the sexually active adult who has had consensual intercourse prior to sexual assault. The implications of microtrauma in the adult are not as conclusive as they are in the child. Published data on adult microtrauma both in "normal" intercourse and following rape are limited.[167, 194, 195] The natural history of microtrauma findings is not precisely known. At the present time, neither culposcopy nor toluidine blue can definitely differentiate rape from consensual coitus, nor can they reliably establish the interval between injury and detection. On balance, both modalities are quite promising and may gain greater clinical significance with further study.

Inspection of the introitus should include a description of the hymen. The hymen is a thin, membranous structure about one millimeter thick, with a connective tissue core and stratified squamous epithelium on each side. Tremendous individual variation in morphology and elasticity exist and can complicate the medical-legal evaluation. If the hymen is intact and uninjured it should be categorized (imperforate, cribiform, anular, semilunar, septate, vertical) and an assessment of elasticity and maximum distensibility made. This last aspect is particularly important because what appears to be an intact hymen with a small opening may stretch to a remarkable degree without injury; a "normal" hymen is, thus, not synonymous with virginity.[15, 35] Any findings of acute trauma are significant and should be carefully documented. When traumatically ruptured, the hymen is often torn posteriorly or in the midline and the remaining remnants, red and bleeding, retract toward the hymenal ring as tender, swollen nubbins. Once torn, the hymen does not regrow and the remnants heal in seven to ten days into small fleshy tags called carnunculae multiformes.[15, 16]

After all the external structures have been examined, the vagina should be inspected. An appropriate sized speculum should be selected and moistened only with water; lubricants are spermicidal and will also alter the assay for acid phosphatase in the vaginal pool fluids.[84] As with vulvar trauma, vaginal injuries are uncommon after coitus in the sexually active adult female. Most vaginal trauma occurs in elderly victims who have dry, atrophic vaginal mucosa and the friction of penile thrusting creates mucosal tears.[15, 16] Foreign objects may produce severe injuries, with penetration into the abdominal cavity. If any intravaginal blood is found, a careful search must be undertaken to distinguish menstrual or uterine bleeding from that secondary to trauma. According to the specifics of the local crime lab protocol, samples should be obtained for acid phosphatase analysis, sperm identification, and the vaginal pool swabbed, aspirated, or lavaged by the examiner to search for motile sperm. Care should be taken to collect fluid from the posterior vault of the vagina and not from the endocervical canal, because intact sperm have been recovered from the cervix up to seventeen days after coitus.[82] Before the speculum is removed, the cervix should be inspected for trauma, parity, signs of early pregnancy, or preexisting infection. A culture for gonorrhea and chlamydia should also be obtained. The bimanual exam should not be omitted because information about tenderness, preexisting pregnancy, or pelvic infection will have significant impact on therapeutic and followup considerations.

If the history gives any indication of sodomy (either attempted or completed) a rectal evaluation should be performed. As with the vulva, the external structures are carefully inspected for any signs of injury or foreign matter. Any suspicious stain should be sampled with a moistened cotton or dacron swab (as previously described). Unlike vulvovaginal injuries after coitus, rectal trauma after anal intercourse is not uncommon; bruising, small eccymoses, and linear lacerations may be found, especially in "anal virgins."[30, 35] Any external trauma necessitates a gentle anoscopic exam with a small, water-moistened anoscope to exclude more serious internal damage. A rectal gonorrhea culture should also be collected. In all cases involving sodomy, it is recommended that the rectum be swabbed with two cotton or dacron swabs and two dry slides prepared. The swabs are then air-dried for sixty minutes in the usual way. Although it is always appropriate to attempt rectal sampling for sperm after sodomy, much controversy exists about both the technique and interpretation of sperm obtained from the rectum.[30, 31, 35] Not only can a number of artifacts (pollen, mucous threads, bacteria) be confused with sperm heads on the permanent slide, but also the finding of sperm (motile or not) must be very carefully interpreted because of the technical problem of obtaining samples from the rectum without contamination from vaginal secretions that have leaked onto the perineum and over the anus.[30, 31] Because of difficulties in interpretation and a generally very low yield of positive findings, some protocols now omit the emergency department evaluation for motile sperm and require only the two dry swabs and slides.

If the victim was forced to perform fellatio (whether or not she is aware of ejaculation) a pharyngeal gonorrhea culture should be taken and slides for sperm obtained. The best place to search for sperm in the oral cavity is behind the upper central incisors.[1, 2] As with the other areas, two air-dried slides (and their corresponding dried swabs) should be taken for permanent staining and evaluation by the criminalist. A sterile, dry, two-inch-by-two-inch gauze pad is then chewed by the victim to obtain a saliva sample; it must be air dried and placed in an appropriately labeled envelope. The saliva will be analyzed to ascertain the victim's antigen secretor status.

The final step in the evidentiary exam is the collection of blood and urine from the victim for laboratory testing. The specific tests and their indications vary from protocol to protocol but generally blood is obtained for syphilis serology (VDRL, RPR), ABO blood group typing, blood alcohol determination, and possibly for serum pregnancy testing (RIA, qualitative β-HCG). Blood and urine for toxicologic screening is sometimes done routinely and sometimes done only with a high index of suspicion. If the victim urinates before the exam, a sample should be saved because it may contain sperm. If the circumstances of the case or local requirements dictate, it may then be sent to the crime lab for analysis. A urine sample is also helpful because the newer beta-HCG monoclonal antibody tests for pregnancy (which are inexpensive, sensitive, and accurate) are rapidly replacing serum HCG tests.

At the conclusion of the history and physical examination the clinician should be prepared to write his or her impressions (see figure 4–5). It is essential to stress the point that the examiner's duty is *not* to judge whether a rape has occurred; rape is a legal entity, not a medical one, and can only be decided upon by the jury.[1, 2, 9, 15, 16] Likewise, the issues of lack of consent, the use of force, and whether the accused person was actually the perpetrator, are all questions that can only be answered by the jury. The examiner's role is limited to rendering an expert opinion on three basic issues.[1, 9, 15, 16, 35] First, a statement should be made as to whether the victim's history is consistent with the exam findings; any discrepancies should be carefully detailed. Second, the record should clearly indicate if any objective medical findings of recent trauma are present. And third, the examiner must decide if there are indications of a recent sexual act. Interpretation of these three opinions must be integrated by the jury into the total body of evidence so they can render the fairest and most objective verdict.

Inappropriate
  Whether a rape has occurred
  Judgments regarding use of force or lack of consent

Appropriate
  Consistency between victim's history and physical exam findings
  Presence of objective medical findings consistent with recent trauma
  Presence of indicia of recent sexual activity

Figure 4–5. *Clinician Assessment following Completion of the Evidentiary Exam*

5
Psychological Impact

Any woman who survives a sexual assault has been through an unforgettable crisis that has the potential to produce a major disruptive influence on her life. Victims almost universally report that the predominant emotion experienced during the assault was fear of death.[6, 32] The violence and intimidation concomitant with rape are usually a much more significant stressor than the sexual aspects of the assault. The victim fears for her life and pays for her freedom with the sexual act. In general, the experience creates a sense of helplessness, intensifies conflicts about dependence and independence, and produces shame and guilt, which may lower self-esteem and hamper trusting relationships, especially with men. Anxiety, feelings of vulnerability, and depression may be persistent problems. Victim response varies depending on life stage, circumstances of the rape, preexisting emotional health, coping style, and support system.

Initial Contact

The victim's initial health care encounter after the assault may have a significant and farreaching impact on her eventual emotional recovery.[53] It is essential that the medical examiner understands the psychodynamics of the rape victim and be aware of the range of emotional responses. Burgess and Holmstrom studied a group of sexual assault victims to assess their needs and expectations during their postrape exam.[61] They found most victims wanted to have a medical examination and be reassured about their physical condition. Many of the women also wanted medical intervention to prevent venereal disease and/or pregnancy. Another group of victims presented to the health care system in search of psychological intervention or emotional support. A small group sought medical attention as a result of outside advice or persuasion; they were ambivalent or unsure about what they expected from the health care encounter. A few victims were so distraught or upset that their primary need was to regain some sense of control.

In addition to having knowledge about the rape victim's unique needs and responses, the examiner should be prepared to offer the necessary support and crisis intervention as indicated. Because of severe distress or preexisting conditions, some victims will require psychiatric consultation in the acute setting. Many communities now have rape crisis counselors available on a twenty-four-hour basis. When possible, this service should be offered to all victims upon initial contact. It is unlikely that emergency department staff members will be involved in any ongoing or long-term therapy, but they should be familiar with local mental health resources and make the appropriate referral. Rape victims who reported the most positive feelings after the medical-legal exam described the medical examiner as one who projected both personal concern and professional objectivity.[61]

Conceptual Models of Victim Response

When confronted with a problem that is complex and poorly understood, a standard scientific approach has been to develop a conceptual model that helps integrate the major elements of the question. The theoretical structure that results provides a framework upon which to begin investigation and analysis. Using the model as a guideline, hypotheses may be generated and tested. Affirmative results confirm the appropriateness of the theory and facilitate refinement. Negative findings necessitate reevaluation and restructuring of the basic model. From a research perspective, the utility of a given model is directly proportional to its overall validity and reliability.

From a clinical standpoint a conceptual model need not be

perfectly accurate or completely applicable to all circumstances to be useful. The psychodynamics of the victim response to sexual assault is a complicated clinical problem to which a number of theoretical models have been applied.[6, 12, 32, 40, 52, 63] None of these models applies to every victim or to every rape. In no way, however, should these theories be considered mutually exclusive. In fact, significant areas of overlap attest to the fact that each addresses the same basic stressor and its resultant responses. For any given case one model may fit better than the others, but detailed understanding of each individual model is generally necessary only for ongoing therapy or for research purposes. A brief review of the common theoretical models that appear in the psychiatric and sexual assault literature is helpful to identify the common denominators (see figure 5–1) and basic principles of the victim responses to rape.

An understanding of these fundamentals is, for a variety of reasons, clearly advantageous to anyone who must interact with the sexual assault victim. Knowledge of the models should demystify the rape experience and help dispel the ubiquitous myths and misconceptions about the victim and the crime. Heightened awareness regarding the psychological impact of the assault sensitizes the provider to the victim's emotional needs and sets the stage for developing an appropriate crisis intervention strategy. Additionally, an informed caregiver is likely to bring less personal anxiety to the

Acute Phase
　Shock
　Disbelief
　Anxiety
　Guilt
　Suppression of true feelings

Recovery Phase
　Depression
　Decreased level of functioning
　Anger
　Integration
　Resolution

Figure 5–1. *Common Denominators in the Emotional Response to Rape*

encounter, which in and of itself affords the victim more effective support. Familiarity with the basic sequence of psychologic events in the aftermath of sexual assault enables the initial provider to fulfill an essential patient education role by alerting the victim to the common emotional sequela of rape. Lastly, the models should create an appreciation for the range of responses experienced by most victims. Identification of outliers, whose reactions are at significance variance from the norm, is essential for immediate evaluation and therapy and to insure optimum mental health followup.

Post Traumatic Stress Disorder

Post Traumatic Stress Disorder (PTSD) has long been known as a clinical entity but only recently has it received formal recognition in the psychiatric literature.[54] This disorder is best known in relation to the multitude of problems suffered by Vietnam veterans, but many sexual assault victims may also have PTSD (see figure 5–2).[49] As defined in the third edition of the American Psychiatric Association's Diagnostic and Statistical Manual of Mental Disorders (DSM–III), Post Traumatic Stress Disorder includes:

Stressors
    Severe and beyond the experience of the victim
    Involve both emotional and physical trauma
    Occur without warning
    Provoke feelings of guilt
    Involve intentional cruelty

Clinical Features
    Re-experiencing the traumatic event (flashbacks, nightmares, intrusive thoughts)
    Blunted responsiveness to the external world
    Restlessness and hyperalertness
    Sleep disorders
    Phobic avoidance to situations that arouse memories of the traumatic event
    Autonomic or emotional lability
    Feelings of guilt

Figure 5–2. *Shared Elements of Post Traumatic Stress Disorder and the Sexual Assault Experience*

... the development of characteristic symptoms after the experiencing of a psychologically traumatic event or events outside the range of human experience usually considered to be normal. The characteristic symptoms involve re-experiencing the traumatic event, numbing of responsiveness to, or involvement with, the external world, and a variety of autonomic, dysphoric or cognitive symptoms.

Any significant stressor can produce PTSD, but it must be severe and beyond the experience of the victim. The most potent stresses are those that involve physical and emotional trauma, occur without warning, provoke feelings of guilt, and involve intentional cruelty. Rape obviously fulfills these requirements. Clinical features of this disorder include the reexperiencing of the traumatic event as manifested by intrusive thoughts, nightmares, or sudden feelings as if the event were reoccurring in response to some triggering stimulus. Victim relationship with the external world is numbed; there is decreased interest, feelings of detachment from others, and constriction of emotional responses. Patients with PTSD may show hyperalertness, have sleep disorders, phobic avoidance to situations that arouse memories of the trauma, or heightening of symptoms in those same situations. Associated features may include depressive symptoms, restlessness, autonomic or emotional lability, and guilt. All these features have been described in sexual assault victims.[6, 12, 32, 49, 50, 52]

Grief Reaction

The sexual assault victim's response to rape has been described as a form of grief reaction.[12, 63, 168] Sudden and unexpected loss produces a fairly characteristic pattern and sequences of emotional and behavioral responses (see table 5–1). Obviously, loss of a loved one is the stereotypic stressor in this model but many other types of loss can provoke acute grief. Loss of a body part, loss of physical functioning, disfigurement, loss of status or identity may all initiate the cascade of grief reactions.[12, 63] The loss experienced by the rape victim may be subtle or covert but nonetheless potent. Some may have been stripped of their sense of security or have lost their trust in society upon which they relied for protection from harm. Others

Table 5–1

Comparison of Models Describing Emotional Response to Rape

Grief[12, 58, 63]	Rape Trauma Syndrome[32]	Response Patterns of Rape Victims[52]
	Acute Phase: Disorganization	*Phase One:* Acute Reaction
Shock	Shock	Shock
Disbelief	Disbelief	Dismay
Fear Feelings of vulnerability	Nonspecific anxiety Feelings: Fear, guilt, self-blame	Anxiety, especially concerning family notification and procedural details of the upcoming medical and legal encounters
Anxiety Increased motor activity	Expressed style: Crying, sobbing, tenseness restlessness, smiling	*Phase Two:* Outward Adjustment
Denial	Controlled style: Outwardly calm	Explanations
Blunted Emotions	True feelings suppressed	Rationalizations
Guilt Self-recrimination	Somatic complaints	Pseudoadjustment with suppression of true feelings

Depression
    Sleep disturbances
    Withdrawal
    Self-imposed social isolation
	Long-term Phase: Reorganization
	
	Increased motor activity
	Depressive symptoms
	Sleep disturbances, nightmares
		Phase Three: Integration and Resolution
		
		Depression
		
		Breakdown of successful defenses of Phase Two

Anger	Phobias Resurfacing of previously suppressed issues	Re-emergence of previously unresolved issues
Integration	Mastery dreams Anger Increased self-esteem and self-reliance	Anger Renewed counseling More realistic self-appraisal Integration

may view their compliance with the assailant's demands with shame and guilt; for many this results in a significant deterioration of self-esteem and self-respect.[63]

The initial phase of grieving often begins with a period of shock, disbelief, or denial. The inescapable reality of the event quickly provokes fear and intense feelings of vulnerability. At this stage victims may report a sense of powerlessness that tends to create anxiety with resultant hyperactivity (pacing, handwringing, compulsive talking, rumination). As the intensity of these early symptoms declines over time, a stage of denial develops. Emotions are blunted; the reality of the event and its consequences are suppressed. Denial eventually gives way to guilt and a collection of "if only . . ." statements. Periods of self-recrimination and inner-directed rage are common. "I should have . . ." statements are also frequent in this stage. As the guilt phase subsides, depression develops with associated sleep disturbances, nightmares, and feelings of hopelessness; withdrawal and self-imposed social isolation may occur.

After a variable length of time, anger begins to replace depression. Anger may initially manifest as outer-directed resentment or hostility toward men in general, the police, the courts, the health care system, or family members.[12] Later in this phase the anger may be more appropriately aimed at the assailant. Anger is usually the last step toward integration of the trauma into perspective with other life experiences. Gradually the victim regains her social and psychological equilibrium. The relative impact of each stage may vary, and some victims may skip or combine stages, but the general features of the grief reaction are very similar to the responses of rape victims.

Rape Trauma Syndrome and Response Patterns

Burgess and Holmstrom have written extensively about the psychodynamic considerations related to rape.[32, 39, 51, 60, 61] Perhaps their best-known work is the description of the Rape Trauma Syndrome (RTS).[32] Their study population encompassed ninety-two adult female victims of sexual assault who presented to Boston City Hospital for postrape evaluation during a one-year period (1972–73). The victims were interviewed initially in the emergency department and followed up by telephone interviews and home visits. Detailed notes of all victim contacts were analyzed for reported systems as well as changes in feelings, thoughts, and behavior.

The authors describe the Rape Trauma Syndrome as an acute stress reaction to a life-threatening situation (attempted or completed forcible rape) with resultant behavioral, somatic, and psychological reactions. The Rape Trauma Syndrome generally occurs in two phases. The first, or acute phase, is a period of disorganization in the victim's lifestyle. The second phase is a long-term process of reorgnization during which the victim gradually integrates the experience and regains her equilibrium.

In the first hours after sexual assault, the victim may experience a wide range of emotions. Victims are commonly overwhelmed by the experience, and often their initial response is shock, disbelief, dismay, or bewilderment. In this "controlled style" the woman may outwardly appear calm, composed, and subdued with her true feelings suppressed or hidden. Other victims may manifest an "expressed style" in which fear or anxiety are shown through crying, sobbing, restlessness, smiling, or tenseness. The medical examiner should be prepared for this spectrum of initial demeanors.

The acute phase of disorganization lasts from a few days to several weeks. As the initial shock of the assault fades, most victims experience an increase in nonspecific anxiety.[52] A variety of resultant somatic complaints may surface. Musculoskeletal symptoms related directly to the trauma sustained during the attack may become a focus of concern or a generalized increase in muscle tension may produce fatigue, headaches, or insomnia. Anxiety may generate a variety of nonspecific gastrointestinal complaints (nausea, anorexia, vague abdominal pain) or genitourinary symptoms (vaginal discharge, vaginal irritation, dysuria, nonspecific pelvic pain).

Acute phase emotional responses are also variable, but the predominant feelings are fear and self-blame. Fear of violence or death is reported almost universally. This reinforces the notion that the strongest effect of the rape experience is related to the forceful, aggressive nature of the act rather than the sexual aspects. Most victims feel some degree of guilt or shame; again, "If only . . ." and "I should have . . ." statements are common. Questions about misinterpreted invitation, unintentional seduction, and loss of ability to control a progressively uncomfortable sexual situation plague many victims. Anxiety and guilt often intensify at the time when the woman must deal with the notification of parents or partners.[52] Socialization and myth in our society continue to foster the assumption that the woman could or should have handled the situation differently to have achieved a better outcome.[50]

Based on work with a smaller number of victims, Sutherland and Scherl have described patterns of response among victims of rape.[52] Their description of the acute reaction and the phase of integration and resolution correlate very well with the Rape Trauma Syndrome formulations of the actue phase and long-term recovery phase (see table 5–1). Sutherland and Scherl's model includes an intermediate phase of "outward adjustment" between the acute and long-term phases. After the initial anxiety and turmoil begin to subside, the victim enters a period of pseudoadjustment in which she returns to seemingly normal functioning at home, school, or work. This outward calmness does not indicate final resolution of the traumatic event and the feelings it has generated. This stage probably correlates with the period of denial discussed in the grief model. The personal impact of the rape is suppressed while the victim gradually deals with her feelings about the assailant. Explanations and rationalizations flourish; victim priority focuses on return to normal functioning rather than gainining insight into or working through her problem. This is also the period when testimony refusal or dropped charges are common.[170] As anxiety lessens and victims feel generally better, many will choose to terminate legal action to avoid the inevitable reemergence of anxiety upon confronting the assailant in court.

The long-term process is labeled "reorganization" by Burgess and Holmstrom and "integration and resolution" by Sutherland and Scherl; both descriptions share several common features (see table 5–1).[32, 52] Several changes occur as the victim eventually comes to terms with the traumatic event she has endured. A general increase in motor activity was observed in many women; changing residence, changing phone numbers, and taking trips (especially to

visit family members not seen daily) were common. A high percentage reported sleep disturbances and nightmares. It's interesting to
note that the nightmares of many victims initially were frighening
replays of the assault associated with intense feelings of helplessness
and being trapped. Over time these gradually evolved to dreams in
which the victims gained mastery of the situation and often
culminated with the death of the assailant.

During this stage a variety of phobias may occur. Traumato-
phobia refers to phobic reactions that develop as a defensive
response to specific traumatic circumstances of the rape. Several
patterns emerged. Women who were attacked in their sleep had a
tendency to develop fear of the indoors. Women who were raped
outside became phobic about being outdoors. Most victims reported
fear of being alone. Many became quite apprehensive in crowds,
especially on public transportation. Victims who had been ap-
proached suddenly by the assailant became fearful of people
walking behind them.

Depressive symptoms and a need to talk were frequently
encountered weeks to months after the attack. Issues that had been
previously suppressed or dealt with superficially resurfaced. Depression during this phase is probably a psychologically normal consequence of the pain involved in resolution and integration of the
experience.[52] Some degree of deterioration in functioning is not
uncommon during this stage as denial fades and the successful
defenses of the intermediate phase weaken. Many victims seek or
renew counseling at this point as they struggle to accept the event
and resolve their feelings about the assailant.

Anger is an unusual response in the acute and intermediate
phases of reaction to sexual assault.[6, 32, 49, 50, 52] The early expression of aggression by the victim may be problematic for several
reasons. Traditional cultural and social standards tend to restrict
females from open displays of anger or hostility; society has
typically expected greater passivity and compliance from women.[169]
To express these feelings engenders the psychological risk of
increasing the victim's guilt because she may subconsciously believe
her anger is indicative of being a "bad person." Suppression of
aggression in the context of sexual assault is arguably adaptive
because the victim is generally smaller and less physically strong

than the assailant. A forceful counterattack may place the victim in considerably greater jeopardy than submission.

The emergence of anger is a healthy and important milestone toward integration and reorganization of the rape experience. As the victim comes to terms with her feelings about her degree of complicity in the rape, emotional energy previously directed inward, which created guilt and self-blame, can now be redirected toward the man who assailed her. As noted above, the first expressions of anger are commonly seen in dreams in which the victim kills or maims the rapist. Along with these feelings of anger the victim may experience an increase in her own sense of self-esteem and self-reliance. When properly recognized and acknowledged these changes can be very helpful adjuncts for victim recovery.

Sexual Dysfunction Following Rape

A variety of sexual problems following rape have been reported (see figure 5–3).[39, 49, 62] The most commonly reported postrape sexual complication was abandonment of all sexual acitivity. Burgess and Holmstrom found that 38 percent of the sexually active victims they studied had not resumed sexual activity at the six-month postassault interview.[39] Another 33 percent of victims described a decrease in sexual activity. Aversion to sex in these women often developed gradually over a period of weeks or months after the attack. The victims who reported no change in sexual frequency not uncommonly complained of some change in their sexual response.

Delayed return to sexual activity
Decreased sexual activity
Altered sexual response
Disruptive flashbacks during sex
Aversion to previously enjoyable sexual acts
Changes in physiological sexual responses (dyspareunia, vaginismus, decreased lubrication)
Difficulty experiencing sexual feelings during intercourse
Orgasmic failure
Intensification of preexisting sexual problems

Figure 5–3. *Potential Sexual Dysfunction in the Female Victim following Sexual Assault*

Flashbacks during sex were frequently reported and often disruptive or distracting. Certain sexual acts that were enjoyable before the rape were described as disgusting or distasteful by some victims after the assault.

Changes in physiologic response created problems for a number of women. Over one-fourth of Burgess and Holmstrom's group complained of dyspareunia secondary to vaginismus and/or decreased vaginal lubrication. Forty-one percent noted difficulty in experiencing any sexual feelings during intercourse or were nonorgasmic. Preexisting sexual problems are likely to be intensified and prolonged by the rape experience. Interestingly, however, prior level of sexual activity did not correlate with the length of recovery. Women who were virgins or not sexually active at the time of the assault may experience a higher frequency of certain symptoms (for example, vaginismus in virginial victims), but their overall length of recovery was not significantly longer than sexually active victims. This also serves to reinforce the contemporary view that the major impact of rape involves more than the sexual features.

Family Response and Support Network

The reaction of the victim's family and partner has a profound influence on her emotional wellbeing and recovery. Families and friends of rape victims tend to behave in some reasonably predictable ways. Families often patronize and overprotect the victim as a means of assuaging their own feelings of guilt and responsibility for failing to adequately protect her.[171] Unfortunately, this behavior may communicate to the victim that her family considers her to be a vulnerable child unable to care for herself. The result is likely to be additional compromise of the victim's already weakened self-esteem and sense of autonomy.

Families may also believe that openly discussing the trauma and the feelings it generates is destructive to the victim because it keeps the painful and anxiety-provoking memories alive. One tactic that serves this notion is to keep the victim continually occupied with activities, trips, and family affairs. Another expression of this belief is the "conspiracy of silence."[171] The victim is encouraged to keep the entire event "secret," ostensibly to protect others from being traumatized by the news. Adherence to this stance eliminates an important resource for victim support and restricts her ability to vent her feelings; it also tends to confirm the woman's fear that what happened is "just too terrible to talk about."

Prior acquaintance with the assailant and/or lack of physical trauma often promote doubts and inhibit the development of a supportive and sympathetic attitude toward the victim. Implications of responsibility or complicity accentuate the victim's feelings of guilt and self-blame. For a number of victims the anticipation of informing parents and/or partner of the assault may generate considerable anxiety.[52] Fears of a generally negative response or outright rejection are often justified and magnify the victim's guilt and shame even further.

In describing the psychological effects and aftereffects of the victims of violence, Symonds notes the widespread tendency of nonvictims to reject the notions of accident, innocence, or random chance in association with violent crime.[63] The belief that victim behavior, either by omission or comission, was in some way responsible for the criminal acts has traditionally been pervasive in the public opinion and in the criminal justice system. Nowhere has this been more problematic than in the area of sex crimes. The reason for this misassigned responsibility, Symonds feels, is a basic need to find some rational explanation for violent crime. A feeling of vulnerability is created by exposure to senseless violence; if any explanation can be produced, those around the victim feel relieved and less vulnerable. Unfortunately, their relief is often at the expense of increasing the victim's anxiety and guilt.

The response of men close to the victim (father, brother, partner) includes several common components.[50] Their masculinity may be threatened by the attack on the woman who "belongs" to them, and by their helplessness and inability (real or perceived) to prevent the assault. The impulse for revenge may be particularly strong and indicative of the male's need to reestablish control and reaffirm the role of protector. Overprotective behavior subsequent to the rape may emerge and serve the same needs. The doubts, suspicions, fantasies, myths, and feelings of helplessness and vulnerability experienced by the victim's sexual partner undoubtedly produces anxiety. It is not uncommon for this anxiety to be of sufficient magnitude to cause the male to withdraw, physically and emotionally, with resultant deterioration of the relationship.

The effect of the responses of family and partners must not be underestimated. The attitudes and reactions of the victim's support network are pivotal in determining the degree and pace of her recovery. A family that is supportive, informed, and knowledgeable about the psychological aftermath of sexual assault will be an invaluable asset during the victim's struggle to regain wellbeing.

Crisis Intervention and Initial Counseling

Even though staff members in the emergency department will not be involved in any long-term counseling of the rape victim, they should be well versed in crisis counseling and intervention. The basic approach should be to steer the victim toward adaptive coping strategies and away from maladaptive behavior. The goal should be to return the woman to normal functioning as soon as possible and to prevent the crystallization of emotional disturbances into psychiatric symptoms.[13, 32] An understanding of the common denominators of emotional response in the postassault period (see figure 5–1) should enable the examiner to provide the necessary support, information, and guidance to help the victim cope with and recover from her ordeal (see figure 5–4).

Nature of the Rape Crisis

A crisis is a turning point in which the individual is confronted with a situation from which escape or avoidance is impossible and usual problem-solving mechanisms are ineffective.[168] A state of intrapsychic disequilibrium results and is punctuated by substantial amounts of anxiety and a deterioration in functioning. The severity and impact of any crisis is shaped by a number of psychological and event-related variables. The individual's degree of vulnerability (as a function of character structure, prior life events, supportive network, and so on) plays a critical role in determining the

Establish rapport and initiate a supportive relationship
    Project calm, attentive demeanor
    Nonverbal support
    Acknowledge victim feelings
Help the victim regain a sense of control
    Encourage (but don't force) the victim to verbalize or write about the affective experience of the assault
    Allow the victim to set the pace and emotional tone of the interview
    Ask permission before examination or evidence collection procedures
Acknowledge fear as the predominant feeling during the attack
    Reassure the victim that she is now safe
    Do not leave the victim alone
Reassure the victim about her physical condition
Inquire about the victim's plans for personal safety and emotional support over the next few days
Acknowledge guilt feelings as universal after rape
    Use generalization, clarification, or reflection to convey understanding and facilitate communication
    Avoid phrases or innuendo that may seem judgmental
Bolster self-esteem and support existing coping skills
    Assure the victim that her real options during the assault were extremely limited
    Offer the perspective that her strength and successful coping abilities facilitated her survival
Attenuate shame and embarrassment
    Start with general questions before moving to more specific inquiries
    Preface sexual questions by explaining the rapist's goal is often to humiliate and degrade the victim
    Balance sexual questions with inquiries about the affective experience
Educate the victim about sexual assault
    Explain the evidentiary procedures
    Prepare the victim for the common psychological and physiological sequela of rape
    Briefly summarize the mechanics of the criminal justice procedures
Educate the family about sexual assault
    Describe common postrape responses from victims and family members
    Disabuse common myths and misconceptions about rape
    Prepare the family for the predictable psychological and somatic sequela the victim is likely to experience
    Warn the family about the regressive consequences of overprotection
    Facilitate a supportive environment for open expression of feelings
    Facilitate appropriate followup

Figure 5–4. *Acute Phase Counseling: Tasks and Techniques*

response. Likewise, the nature and unexpectedness of the precipitating event can vary considerably with the resultant effect proportional to the severity of the insult. The individual's preexisting coping skills and how effectively they are applied during the crisis and immediately afterward are critical in determining where the individual begins along the response spectrum.

The crisis state produced by sexual assault results when an external traumatic force ruptures intrapsychic homeostasis and disturbs the balance between adaptive capacity and the environment. In addition to the elements common to all forms of crisis, the rape experience engenders some unique features and special considerations. The amount and character of the violence and the victim's relationship to the assailant may have significant influence on the degree of stress generated.[170] The presence of unrelated but concurrent stresses in the victim's life affects her ability to deal with the aftermath of sexual assault. The responses from those close to the victim often have a profound impact. The reactions from family and partner are especially significant when viewed within the context of the ubiquitous myths, misconceptions, and stigmatization surrounding rape.

Rape is an intense and violent invasion of innermost personal space that threatens the integrity of bodily boundaries. The degree of insult to the self in sexual assault is probably surpassed only by homicide.[12, 169] Victims overwhelmingly report fear of injury or death as the predominant feeling during the assault.[6, 32, 49, 50, 51, 60, 169] The price for survival and freedom is the sexual act. The woman often becomes the faceless object for the expression of the rapist's hostility. Sex is his weapon. Victims feel used and degraded; they describe this experience as depersonalizing and dehumanizing.[169]

Despite these realities, society tenaciously continues to view rape as primarily sexual. Those who interact with the victim after the assault (police, health care personnel, family, friends) tend to reinforce this attitude by focusing on the sexual aspects of the crime. The message received by the victim is subtle but persistent: Rape is a sexual encounter gone awry; she could or should have handled the situation differently for a better outcome. The resultant victim affects of shame and guilt are nearly universal.[6, 12, 49, 50, 52, 169, 170] When these self-deprecating feelings are combined with the apparent disapproval from those around her, she is often left with a sense of isolation and alienation.

Most people share the deepseated belief that bad things only happen to others. Any crisis forces a confrontation between this idealized view of the world and reality. For the sexual assault victim the breakdown of her usual existential denial of environmental threats creates intense feelings of vulnerability and helplessness.[168] Anxiety, phobias, and fear, to the point of paranoid ideation, may restrict the victim's activity and significantly alter the ways in which she relates to the space around her. For many victims the assault represents loss of control and usually results in a painful sense of psychic disorganization.

These same feelings of powerlessness and lack of control may also affect the victim's interpersonal relationships. The sexual assault experience often intensifies conflicts in relationships.[169] Trusting relationships with men may be hampered, especially if the rape occurred in the context of a social encounter. The victim's family may view her not as an adult but as a vulnerable child needing guidance and protection. Their behavior, coupled with the victim's guilt and sense of helplessness, may provoke regression and further undermine her already limited sense of self-worth. Conflicts about dependence and independence may linger.

Life Stage Considerations

The age and life circumstances of the sexual assault victim are important variables that must be carefully considered to adequately understand her response and to formulate the best counseling plan. Different life stages engender different psychodynamic issues; the clinician must be sensitive to these unique needs and concerns of the victim.

The largest victim group is composed of young, single women between seventeen and twenty-four years of age.[50, 169] This type of victim is typically a novice at being on her own and is often relatively inexperienced in dealing with the world in general and men in particular. For many of these women the rape occurs when she becomes enmeshed in an unwelcome sexual encounter with a man she knows. The consequent guilt and shame may be particularly overwhelming. Her concerns about separation from family and independence may create significant stress and anxiety. Well-intentioned support and care-giving by the young victim's family is likely to reinforce her feelings of inadequacy and foster regression, thus delaying or preventing mastery of the turmoil evoked by the assault.[169]

The divorced or separated woman is at great risk of having her credibility questioned. The stigma of being a divorcee includes societal assumptions of loose morality and sexual availability. She is presumed to possess the experience and savvy the younger victim lacks. These attitudes magnify the victim's feelings of self-recrimination from her inability to control the situation. Her sense of adequacy and ability to function independently are threatened. If she is a single parent, her capacity to care for and protect her children may be challenged.

The middle-aged married victim may be subjected to some unique stresses as a result of sexual assault. She is probably already at a point of critical reassessment of her life role as she struggles with her "empty nest" and the changed relationships with her now-adult children. Her anxieties about the preexisting issues of self-worth, independence, and sexual adequacy may be intensified after the assault. As a potential compounding factor, her husband may be engulfed in his own midlife crisis and hence be less able to respond to and support his wife's escalating emotional needs.

Acute Phase Counseling: Goals and Objectives

The general goal of any crisis intervention is to restore the patient to his or her prior level of functioning.[32, 49, 169, 170] This includes a return to the previous degree of adaptation and relationship to the social environment. If baseline functioning is seriously impaired (that is, the patient is psychotic, borderline, or suicidal) the level of intervention must be increased appropriately to provide psychiatric consultation, medication, hospitalization, or any other resource that is indicated.

The goals of counseling in the acute aftermath of rape must address both intrapsychic disorganization and environmental realities. In the immediate postassault period the victim is barraged with a number of practical matters requiring decisions or action. She must make determinations about medical care and police involvement. Physical security precautions must be attended to and she must decide whether and how to tell family and friends about the assault. The victim probably feels overwhelmed and vulnerable; she needs an atmosphere that conveys safety and offers the support necessary to help her collect her thoughts and organize her plan of action.

Another phychological objective in the acute phase is helping the victim regain some sense of control. Efforts directed at bolstering her self-esteem and restoring some measure of self-confidence will be beneficial by attenuating her acute anxiety and guilt. A very important objective of the initial health care encounter after sexual assault is the education of the patient and her family about the psychodynamics and common psychological sequela of the rape experience. This information will help demystify sexual assault for all involved and aid the victim by enlisting the family as adjunct counselors. After a sound therapeutic foundation has been laid by crisis intervention and patient education, it is essential to provide her with access to the appropriate counseling resources for further care.

Acute Phase Counseling: Tasks and Techniques

Logically, the first steps toward a successful interaction should be the nurturing of rapport and the initiation of a supportive relationship. Projecting a demeanor that is calm, concerned, and attentive conveys empathy and reassures the victim that she is not being rejected or doubted. Nonverbal support, such as offering coffee or a blanket, may be very effective and gratefully received. Acknowledging victim feelings with empathetic statements (such as, "you must feel drained and exhausted") demonstrates understanding and promotes rapport. Early in the encounter it is quite advantageous to identify the victim's main concerns and assess her perception of the kind of help she needs. This reassures the victim that help is at hand and facilitates communication.

The content, structure, and pace of the interview have important and farreaching ramifications. Obviously, a primary objective of the interview is to gather a complete and accurate history from the victim. Data collection, however, is not the only consequence. A well-conducted encounter not only optimizes the quality and quantity of information transmitted to the medical examiner but also offers rich potential for helping the victim emotionally and psychologically. Unfortunately, the converse is also true; a poorly conducted interview at best produces a substandard history and at worst magnifies her anxiety and guilt and complicates her recovery. Application of basic principles and a few common techniques can greatly benefit both the interviewer and the victim.

The sense of helplessness and loss of control that most victims feel require patience and support. Encouraging her to talk about the assault, especially the affective experience, enhances self-control and facilitates mastery over the stress and anxiety. Allowing the victim to set the pace and emotional tone of the interview also helps her regain a sense of control. A forceful interrogation or attempts to push for a catharsis are likely to be psychologically reminiscent of the assault and result in accentuated feelings of helplessness and anxiety. A heavy-handed approach may also undermine her existing coping skills and cause further decompensation.[170] If the victim is having difficulty talking about the assault, a useful technique to employ is to have her write down what she remembers about the details of the attack and her feelings during and after the rape.[6] This method of interviewing not only decreases anxiety and bolsters self-control but may provide a valuable document for subsequent legal proceedings.

Fear of death or injury and resultant feelings of vulnerability are almost uniformly reported by sexual assault victims. It is therapeutic to acknowledge this fear as extremely intense and universal during and immediately after rape. The victim should be reassured that she is now in a safe environment. She should not be left alone since this may heighten her anxiety and sense of vulnerability. Most women are concerned about bodily integrity and gain solace after the clinician has completed the examination and has given reassurance about physical health issues. At the close of the medical-legal encounter it is prudent and comforting to inquire about the victim's plans for personal safety and emotional support during the next few days.

Most rape victims are troubled by feelings of guilt after the assault. "If only. . . ." and "I should have . . ." statements are characteristic of perceived culpability and should be recognized and discussed. Generalization and clarification are useful interview techniques that improve communication and demonstrate understanding. For example: "Many rape victims think they could or should have done something differently to prevent the attack. Do you feel that way?" Or, the interviewer might reflect: "It sounds as though you feel partially responsible for what happened. Is that a concern you have?" Such statements acknowledge and legitimize victim feelings and open the door for discussion and eventual mastery. It is especially important for the interviewer to cautiously avoid phrases or innuendo that might seem suspicious or judgmental, because they only increase the victim's feelings of self-blame.

Closely associated with guilt are lowered self-esteem and impaired self-confidence. Victims often berate themselves for handling the situation in an inadequate or ineffective way. An excellent supportive tactic is to affirm that the victim's strength and successful coping abilities in this dangerous situation were responsible for her survival. Hindsight frequently provokes victim speculation about what she could have done if she were "braver, stronger, or less afraid." She should be reassured that in reality her options were extremely limited and her compliance was both necessary and appropriate.

The rape experience, especially the sexual aspects, may generate considerable embarrassment, shame, and humiliation. These emotions probably deter many women from reporting the crime. Those who do report are faced with the unpleasant task of telling and retelling the sexually explicit details of the assault to a number of strangers (policeman, nurse, physician, counselor) and finally to a whole courtroom.

In the acute aftermath of the attack, the victim is already anxious and guiltridden. Initially focusing the interview on the sexual aspects of the assault tends to increase both anxiety and self-recrimination. A more functional approach is to begin with general questions and move gradually to more specific issues. Before exploring the sexual material, preface that portion of the history by telling the victim that the rapist's aim may be to degrade and humiliate the woman. Explain that these matters, although difficult to discuss, are essential to guide the examination and evidence collection; the more accurate and complete this information is, the better the victim's chances to obtain justice. The victim may become less reticent about discussing the intimate sexual details of the assault if she understands the fact that each act may engender separate charges and therefore a longer cumulative sentence. Another technique that helps reduce the anxiety associated with the sexual history is to balance sexual questions with inquiries about the victim's affective responses to the violence and fear associated with the rape.

Educating the Victim

Victim education is interwoven throughout the entire postassault period and has two main focuses. Very early in the encounter it is essential to assist the victim in regaining a sense of control and some predictability in her environment. The interviewer should carefully and clearly summarize the sequence of events in the upcoming evidentiary exam. A brief explanation about the components of the examination and evidence collection procedure will improve victim cooperation and lessen anxiety. It is also very beneficial for the victim to understand exactly what is expected of her during the exam and what her responsibilities for followup include. Restoration of control is enhanced by asking the victim's permission before the various exam maneuvers and evidence collection tasks.

The second educational focus is best deferred until near the end of the evidentiary examination process when some rapport has developed and the victim feels a bit more organized. It is at this point that the interviewer can begin to prepare the victim for what she is likely to experience over the days and weeks ahead. A useful technique is to review with the victim one of the models of the emotional response to rape described previously (see table 5–1). This information should be in synopsis form and prefaced with an explanation that work with other sexual assault victims has shown that many women experience similar stresses and emotions in the aftermath of rape. The victim should understand that she as a unique individual may not fit the pattern exactly but the general knowledge about what others in her situation have gone through is likely to help lessen her anxiety and fear about the unknown. A brief, clearly written summary describing the common denominators of the rape response patterns augments the discussion and serves as reinforcement and support for the victim after she goes home.

In addition to information regarding the psychological experiences and work ahead, the victim needs an accurate and realistic appraisal about the police investigation and court procedures. Again, fear of the unknown is at issue. These data are also necessary to assist the victim in making informed decisions during her involvement with the criminal justice system. This information is generally supplied by the responding police officer and the district attorney, but the interviewer should be sufficiently versed to at least outline the basics and answer commonly asked questions.

At the close of the encounter the interviewer should enlighten the victim about the options available to her for support, information, and counseling. This approach should convey a sense of hope and encourage the victim to believe that she can and will feel better. It is important to help mobilize her toward the appropriate resources, but a word of caution is in order. With well-intentioned zeal to be helpful and reassuring, family, friends, or health care personnel may inadvertently regress the victim by telling her what to do or by doing everything for her. The message the victim may receive is that she really is incapable of taking care of herself; passivity and dependence are elicited and her guilt and lowered self-esteem may worsen. The interviewer must encourage the victim to take an active role in her recovery and in the numerous decisions to be made after sexual assault.

Symptom Management

As discussed previously, the anxiety of the acute phase may generate a variety of somatic and emotional complaints. These

symptoms may be "psychological bandages" that serve as emergency methods to contain the anxiety that threatens further
disorganization.[170] Physical complaints are often nonspecific and
unexplained by direct injury. These include headaches, muscle
tension, fatigue, vague gastrointestinal distress, or nonspecific genitourinary symptoms.[32, 52] For individuals who characteristically
somaticize as a way of expressing emotional turmoil, the symptoms
produced tend to be more troublesome, less well defined, or more
persistent. Medical investigation of these problems should be as
thorough as necessary to reassure the patient and the clinician that
a significant organic basis is absent. Generally, reassurance alone is
the best and most appropriate therapy. It is often helpful to gently
and supportively explain the normal relationship between emotional stress and physical symptoms. It is essential that this information be conveyed in a nonthreatening and nonjudgmental
fashion. If the victim with somatic discomfort leaves the encounter
feeling the medical examiner has perceived her as "crazy" or a
"crock" she will lose even more self-esteem and probably face a
longer and more difficult recovery.

The emotional dysphoria inherent in the rape experience covers
the spectrum from mild to incapacitating. The common denominator, especially in the immediate postassault period, is generalized
anxiety.[32, 49, 52, 54] Victims may be restless or tense; they may
exhibit an exaggerated startle response. Many report difficulty
concentrating and lability of affect. Intrusive thoughts may be very
disruptive and insomnia may further tax physical and emotional
reserves. The foundation of therapy for these problems is a support
network that is empathetic, patient, and understanding. In the acute
setting of the emergency department evidentiary exam it may, on
occasion, be appropriate to prescribe a short course of an anxiolytic
or sedative agent.

Several caveats about drug therapy following rape are in order.
Victims with significant preexisting psychiatric or social difficulties
may decompensate when confronted with the stresses of sexual
assault. A severely distraught rape victim merits further evaluation
to rule out a "compound reaction." Minor tranquilizers used for
anxiety in this situation may be ineffective, may delay accurate

diagnosis, or may even exacerbate a more serious subterranean psychiatric illness.

Uncomplicated patients who are appropriate candidates for a brief course of anxiolytics should be cautioned about two points. First, although these drugs promote a sense of wellbeing by decreasing the discomfort associated with feeling anxious, they tend to interfere with the working-through process. In the long run, mastering anxiety requires time and skillful counseling, not chemicals. Second, the victim must be made aware that, despite the best intentions from all concerned, pharmacologic therapy for anxiety risks the development of a dysfunctional feedback loop. Medication brings temporary relief but not resolution. The danger is that the patient will repetitively opt for the "quick fix" with multiple requests for drugs and fail to obtain or pursue counseling.

Most victims experience some depressive feelings after sexual assault. The predominant affects in the acute phase are fear, anxiety, guilt, and shame.[169] Mild depressive symptoms are also common immediately after rape and may be manifested as tearful or withdrawn behavior. Other acute symptoms such as restlessness, agitation, self-deprecation, or insomnia may overlap with anxiety or guilt. Major depression, however, is unusual in the acute phase and when present or suspected should raise the question of a compound reaction. Mild depression should be treated supportively; significant depression, especially if it involves delusional or suicidal thinking, warrants psychiatric evaluation for hospitalization and/or medication.

The resurgence of depression is quite common during the recovery phase weeks to months after the attack. Depression at this stage is probably a psychologically normal response to the pain associated with resolution of the experience as the victim comes to terms with her relationship to the assailant and the personal significances of the assault.[52] Renewing or reaffirming the counseling relationship is the fundamental therapeutic approach at this point. Specific antidepressant therapy is seldom indicated but if contemplated should be done so with psychiatric consultation. Obviously it is unlikely that this issue will confront the initial medical examiner.

Facilitating Effective Support from Family
and Partner

The victim's support network, especially her family and mate, plays a crucial role in her recovery. The spectrum of impact is quite broad, varying from extremely negative and destructive to immeasurably positive and therapeutic. The initial health care encounter following sexual assault offers a unique and fertile opportunity to mobilize the family as a constructive resource. A relatively small time investment during this critical period may pay significant long-term dividends in assisting the victim to regain her emotional balance.

Rape is undeniably a disruptive and traumatic event in the life of the victim. Rape is also a potent stressor for those close to the victim and frequently precipitates a crisis and threatens the psychological equilibrium of her couple and family systems.[171] Family members may experience the same affective responses of shock, vulnerability, shame, and guilt that the victim feels. It is essential to recognize that the victim's support network is also in crisis and will need some degree of acute counseling or intervention.

Individuals close to the victim are vulnerable to all the prejudices, misconceptions, and myths about sexual assault that are so prevalent in public opinion. Families often react more to the sexual component of the attack than to the inherent violence and threat to life. The anger, guilt, and helplessness they feel may be manifested by doubt, suspicion, overprotectiveness, or even open hostility.[171] If such attitudes and emotions go on unchecked they may provoke a "revictimization" of the woman by prolonging and exacerbating her intrapsychic dysharmony.

With the victim's permission, a few minutes spent with the family and partner is likely to be beneficial.[171] The focus of this initial encounter is primarily didactic but in some circumstances may also include a measure of crisis intervention or psychotherapeutic counseling. The first task is to begin demystifying sexual assault by explaining the violent nature of rape and stress the fact that the victim's perception of the attack is dominated by the aggression and threat to life, not the sexual aspects. Educating the family about the other common emotions experienced by victims following rape (fear, guilt, shame, vulnerability) is an important step toward disabusing common misconceptions. Specific issues or questions about the rape experience should be dealt with in a factual, authoritative, and nonjudgmental fashion.

The next task is to prepare the family for the common psychological and somatic sequela of sexual assault. Just as previously done for the victim, sharing with the family a brief synopsis of one of the response models (such as rape trauma syndrome; see table 5–1) decreases anxiety, reinforces demystification, and lays a solid foundation for functional support in the weeks and months ahead.

Optimally, the victim's family and mate are motivated to assist her through this crisis and back to her previous level of functioning and wellbeing. This desire to help should be acknowledged and directed toward productive strategies. An important part of this task is to convey to the family the degree of responsibility they share in creating a successful recovery for the victim. This task offers an excellent opportunity to educate the family about the common, but dysfunctional, tactics (overprotection, distraction, conspiracy of silence) often employed by well-meaning but misguided relatives and spouses. They must understand that they can be most productive in their efforts when they assist the victim in mobilizing her own best coping skills as an independent adult rather than a vulnerable child. They must support her with understanding and empathy and avoid the sometimes overwhelming desire to take control by making decisions for her and smothering her with a cloak of overprotection.

The final task is to teach the family about the importance of creating a safe and supportive environment into which both they and the victim can release troubling thoughts and feelings. They need to clearly understand that open expression of feelings, however disturbing, is fundamental to achieve mastery and resolution of this shared crisis. The atmosphere must remain empathetic and noncritical; emotions and thoughts must be allowed to flow freely but not forced. The victim's support network should be reassured that there is not a single "right" thing to say or do, but that their open and nonjudgmental caring affords the best chance for a timely and successful recovery.

Ongoing Therapy and Long-term Followup

Obviously, the health care team that initially evaluates and treats the victim after the assault is not likely to be involved in her continuing therapy. Their initial efforts in crisis intervention and acute phase counseling should lay the groundwork for subsequent therapy both in the context of the victim's support network and in a more formal mental health setting. The issues and techniques germane to ongoing therapy for rape victims are beyond the scope of this book. The final task of the evidentiary exam team is to guide the victim toward the most appropriate psychological followup.

Most women are probably mentally healthy and functioning normally before the assault, and do not require psychiatric care. Some victims who exhibit severe reactions or have significant social or emotional problems prior to the rape require acute psychiatric evaluation. Every victim can benefit from some form of crisis counseling after sexual assault. Nearly all communities have now organized some type of rape crisis or support group to aid the victims of sexual crimes. These groups are generally successful in helping victims by decreasing their sense of isolation, reaffirming the strength of existing coping skills, and offering a knowledgeable support system to augment the resources of family and friends.

6
Forensic Evaluation

I n most communities the health care provider who performs the medical-legal exam on the rape victim is not a forensic pathologist or trained criminalistics specialist. It is, therefore, unlikely that the medical examiner will either be involved in the actual laboratory evaluation of assault-related specimens or be asked to testify as an expert in forensic science. However, it is helpful if everyone responsible for evidence collection has a basic familiarity with the limitations and potential benefits to be expected from the crime lab analysis of physical evidence submitted from the postassault exam.

From a forensic standpoint, the main responsibilities of the evidence collector (physician or nurse) are twofold. As previously discussed, strict adherence to "chain of evidence" procedure is mandatory to insure the integrity of results and admissibility in court. The other area of concern is meticulous attention to the details of evidence collection and preservation as set forth in local protocols from the district attorney's office and from the crime lab. Sloppy technique can produce inaccurate, invalid, and unreliable results, which could destroy an otherwise solid case.

Sexual assault is a perfect example of Locard's principle, which states: "every contact leaves a trace."[35] The physical and usually violent nature of the crime affords ample opportunity for evidence to be transferred to the victim or to the assailant, or left at the scene. Clothing, foreign material (fibers, hairs, soil, plant matter), and biologic samples (blood, saliva, semen, feces, urine) may be recovered and analyzed. Clothing or bed linen may actually yield more significant evidence than specimens taken from the victim. As an example, semen stains from the victim's underwear may contain more evidence material and be less contaminated than swabs collected from her vagina. For the criminalist, each evidence sample represents a piece of scientific data. With skill and experience these pieces can be assembled to support an objective reconstruction of the event.

Corroboration

The crime lab is most helpful in the area of corroboration. Rape is rarely witnessed by anyone except the victim and the perpetrator(s). The resultant legal dilemma will rapidly deteriorate into one person's word against another's without corroborating evidence to substantiate or refute the various versions of the event.

There are three parts of the sexual assault investigation that can be illuminated by forensic laboratory data (see figure 6–1). The first is in the area of consent. The general concept of consent as it relates to the use of force and victim resistance is a complex legal problem. A special facet of this issue addressed in the forensic evaluation is the victim's ability to grant lawful consent for sexual activity. In most protocols a victim's blood alcohol level is determined routinely and blood/urine toxicology is performed if there is clinical suspicion of drug ingestion. Documented intoxication may preclude lawful consent.

The second area is the corroboration of whether the sexual contact actually took place. Identification of seminal constituents, although not technically mandatory, is functionally very important in the preparation of any case if prosecution is anticipated.

Quantitate intoxication with drugs or alcohol that may have invalidated lawful consent

Confirm the occurrence of a recent sexual act by demonstrating the presence of seminal constituents

Include or exclude potential suspects based on evaluation of trace evidence collected from the victim, the assailant, and the crime scene

Figure 6–1. *Objectives of the Forensic Laboratory Evaluation of Suspected Sexual Assault in the Adult Female Victim*

The third aspect, suspect identification/elimination, has undergone rapid technological advancement in recent years. Research in the forensic applications of genetic markers has added a powerful dimension to the laboratory evaluation of rape. Even small amounts of evidence material may be sufficient to construct a genetic profile of the assailant. The value of this profile is mainly exclusionary and may significantly restrict the suspect population. The comparison of the genetic typing from the assailant (ascertained from material left behind and subsequently collected during the examination of the victim) and from a potential suspect may definitely exclude that suspect or, conversely, offer the prosecutor a substantial element in the case against him.

The emerging technology of genetic engineering has recently been applied to the forensic evaluation of rape. It has now been shown that DNA recovered from sperm obtained from evidence material can be analyzed to reveal a specific pattern of DNA fragments.[174, 175] The patterns are unique to the individual; these "DNA fingerprints" may conclusively identify or exclude a suspect. At present, this technology still lies in the realm of research but it offers realistic potential to revolutionize the genetic profiling of forensic evidence.

Identification of Semen

The presence of seminal constituents in the vagina of the female is considered conclusive evidence that intercourse has occurred.[70, 81] Semen can be detected by a variety of laboratory tests. Some markers are specific for semen (not found in any other bodily tissue or fluid), so their presence in any amount is confirmatory. The two members of this group are spermatozoa and the seminal plasma glycoprotein p30. A number of other substances are found in high concentrations in semen but also produced in smaller quantities in other tissues. When the quantitative values of these substances exceed threshold levels, semen is presumed to be present. The best-studied and most commonly used member of this group is acid phosphatase (ACP). Other seminal components that may be helpful in certain cases included choline, spermine, gamma glutamyl transpeptidase (GGT), leucine aminopeptidase (LAP), and zinc.[21, 70, 146, 150]

Obviously, a positive finding only confirms that a sexual act took place, not that a rape has been committed. Conversely, the absence of ejaculatory material disproves neither coitus nor rape.

Some forensic investigators have reported that no evidence of semen was found in 25 percent to 30 percent of otherwise well-substantiated rape cases.[146, 147, 148] A number of factors besides false accusation may account for negative seminal findings (see figure 6–2). Sexual dysfunction among rapists, including ejaculatory failure, has already been discussed.[36] Condom use by the assailant is unusual but certainly possible. Probably the most common cause of negative results is a time delay of sufficient duration between the sexual act and the collection of specimens, which allows for the loss of seminal material beyond the limits of reliable laboratory measurement and analysis.[72] Phagocytosis and enzymatic degradation account for some of the loss but by far the most significant factor is drainage of material from the victim's vagina secondary to upright body position. This fact reinforces the importance of analyzing whatever fabric was closest to the victim's perineum after the assault (underwear, nightgown, bed linen, etc.). Dilution of evidence material from endogenous vaginal secretions or from patient hygiene efforts (douching or bathing) may also hinder the forensic evaluation.

Spermatozoa

Because spermatozoa are a unique marker for semen, their detection is of obvious interest in the investigation of sexual assault. The

Sexual dysfunction (such as ejaculatory failure) in the assailant
Condom use by the assailant
Significant time delay between assault and exam
  Degradation of seminal components
  Drainage of material
  Dilution from endogenous secretions
Patient hygiene (such as douching, washing, bathing, etc.)

Figure 6–2. *Factors that May Limit the Recovery or Detection of Seminal Constituents from the Adult Female Sexual Assault Victim*

initial evaluation for sperm from surface stains or from within body cavities is readily accomplished by using basic equipment available in the emergency department. An immediate wet mount examination of any suspicious material is generally the responsibility of the emergency department examiner. This same material is later stained selectively for spermatozoa and reviewed by the criminalist. Because discrepancies have been reported between the emergency department findings and the subsequent crime lab evaluation for sperm, it is essential that the exact same slides are independently studied.[178] Many factors may influence the findings, so any interpretation of the results must be cautiously integrated with the specific details of the individual case.

In addition to the factors that limit recovery of all seminal components, a number of other items may decrease the probability of finding sperm (see figure 6–3).[15, 27, 65, 68] Decreased or absent spermatogenesis creates oligospermia or aspermia and may be due to congenital abnormalities (germinal aplasia or hypoplasia, cryptorchidism), hormonal deficiencies (hypothyroidism, hypopituitarism, hypogonadism), testicular irradiation, drugs (such as cancer chemotherapy), neoplasm, varicocele, or infection (such as mumps, tuberculosis, gonorrhea). Elevated scrotal temperature (frequent hot baths, tight clothing) may decrease sperm production.[15] Any

Any factor that limits the detection of seminal constituents in general (figure 6–2)
Impaired spermatogenesis
   Germinal aplasia or hypoplasia
   Hormonal deficiencies (pituitary, thyroid, gonadal)
   Testicular irradiation
   Drugs/chemicals (cancer chemotherapy, pesticides, etc.)
   Neoplasm
   Varicocele
   Infection (mumps, tuberculosis, gonorrhea)
   Elevated scrotal temperature
   Chronic alcoholism
Depleted stores (frequent ejaculation) may contribute to intermittent azoospermia
Impaired delivery
   Congenital abnormalities
   Trauma
   Surgery (such as vasectomy)

Figure 6–3. *Factors that May Limit the Recovery or Detection of Spermatozoa from the Adult Female Sexual Assault Victim*

congenital abnormality, trauma, or surgery (such as vasectomy) that anatomically interrupts the flow of sperm will obviously be clinically significant. All of these factors are uncommon but must be kept in mind when evaluating the specifics of an individual case.

Frequent ejaculation in the period just before the sample in question may deplete stores of mature spermatozoa and yield an ejaculate devoid of sperm.[65] The point to be stressed here is that an individual may be intermittently azoospermic (semen devoid of sperm).[147] No conclusion is possible when the suspect's semen contains sperm but the assault material revealed semen without evidence of sperm.

A recently recognized, but probably very common cause of decreased or absent sperm, is chronic alcoholism.[27] Cirrhosis or testicular atrophy need not be present. The postulated mechanism involves a "relative" vitamin A deficiency secondary to the influence of alcohol dehydrogenase (ADH) on vitamin A metabolism with resultant depressed spermatogenesis.

In light of the many factors influencing the recovery of spermatozoa from sexual assault case material, two caveats regarding interpretation of findings deserve emphasis. First, a positive finding from the emergency department wet mount should be confirmed by the permanently stained slides. And second, a negative finding (no sperm detected by either technique) is not helpful. Just as with semen generally, the absence of spermatozoa disproves neither consensual coitus nor rape.

Sperm Motility

Assuming that a sexual act has taken place, that ejaculation has occurred, that semen has been deposited, and that sperm are present in the semen, an assessment of sperm motility is helpful. Objective evidence that quantifies the time interval between the most recent sexual act and the evidentiary exam is crucial for corroboration. Specific methods for estimating the postcoital interval are discussed in the next section.

It is generally agreed that the least equivocal laboratory test for confirming recent ejaculation is the direct wet mount observation of motile sperm.[15, 21, 23, 24, 29, 44, 68] It has been estimated that, on the average, about 80 percent of sperm in the normal, healthy adult male are motile at the time of ejaculation.[15, 65] Thereafter, motility declines very rapidly with the rate of decay and the longevity of motile individuals affected by many variables (see figure 6–4).

Immature or abnormal sperm in the ejaculate tend to lose motility sooner than normal sperm.[73, 83] Motility fluctuates in relation to the menstrual phase.[15, 18, 65] Sperm deposited during the first half of the cycle (days 1–14) show greater longevity and motility than those deposited in the second half or luteal phase.[44] This is especially true for sperm emitted to menstrual effluvium (usually days 1–5), which may surpass average motility by 25 percent.[65, 66]

The vaginal mileu may also compromise motility. Infections (gardnella, trichomonas, monilia, *E. coli*) and vaginal pH below 6.0 both decrease sperm viability.[15, 65] Contraceptive jellies, creams, and suppositories, as well as water soluble lubricants, will also limit motility.[84] It has been suggested that circulating antibodies may develop in the female that recognize spermatozoa as antigenic and prematurely inactivate and kill them.[15, 145]

Anatomic location of the spermatozoa within the female genital tract also has influence on both motility and morphological survival. In general, sperm may remain motile in the fallopian tubes up to forty-eight hours with anecdotal reports to two and one-half weeks.[65, 66, 69] Survival and motility in the uterus is usually twenty-four to forty-eight hours.[65, 66, 69] These findings are more important in relation to fertility than in the medical-legal evaluation

Prolonged Motility Time
    Deposition into cervical mucous at midcycle
    Deposition into menstrual effluvium
    Deposition during follicular phase of menstrual cycle (days 1–14)

Decreased Motility Time
    Immature or immobile sperm
    Vaginal infections
    Vaginal pH less than 6.0
    Spermacidal contraceptives
    Water soluble lubricants
    Female antibodies (?)

Figure 6–4. *Factors Affecting Duration of Sperm Motility*

of the female rape victim, because sampling above the cervix is technically more difficult and not routinely done.

The forensic evaluation of the live rape victim has generated much interest concerning the fate of sperm in the lower female genital tract (cervix and vagina). Unfortunately, there is little uniformity on this subject in the medical and forensic literature. Methodological differences abound and unreferenced anecdotes are common. Wecht and Collom have pointed out the pitfalls of comparing data obtained from evidentiary exams and volunteer-based fertility studies, because the amount of vaginal secretion and its chemical constituents affect sperm vitality and vary considerably with degree of sexual excitement.[70] Based on somewhat limited data, other investigators have found fairly good correlation between volunteer studies and case material.[150]

Estimating the Postcoital Interval

Most postassault exam protocols call for sampling of the vaginal pool (usually the posterior fornix) by swab, aspiration, or saline lavage and immediate wet mount examination for evidence of motile sperm. If available, a phase contrast microscope greatly facilitates the identification of motile sperm by "optical staining."[70] At trial it is likely the examiner will be asked to describe the findings and discuss their medical implications. If motile sperm are seen, an estimation of the coital-examination interval will probably be requested.

If any generalization from the literature review on the subject is possible, it is that sperm motility in the postcoital vagina averages two to four hours.[15, 22, 23, 65, 66, 67, 68] It should be stressed that the confidence limits for the "average" interval are relatively broad. There is even less agreement on the upper time limits of motility (see table 6–1). Variation in maximum reported motility intervals also affects calculated averages.

In his exhaustive review, Pollak noted that motile sperm were found in the vagina up to twenty-eight hours after coitus.[65] Based on "an extensive review of the literature and years of experience by the staff of the Attorney-General's Laboratory for Ontario," Sharpe found motile forms in the vagina up to six hours after coitus.[66]

Table 6–1

Maximum Reported Recovery Times for Spermatozoa
Recovered from the Lower Female Genital Tract

Vagina	Motile	Nonmotile	
Pollack[65]	28 hours	Davies & Wilson[21]	6 days
Sharpe[66]	6 hours	Soules[23]	3 days*
Rupp[67]	8 hours	Silverman & Silverman[24]	10 days**
Wallace-Haagens[69]	12 hours	Morrison[44]	9 days
Massey[71]	6 hours	Sharpe[66]	4 days
		Rupp[67]	14 hours
		Wallace-Haagens[69]	2 days***
		Willot & Allard[148]	26 hours (Head & Tail)
			5 days (Heads only)

Cervix	Motile	Nonmotile	
Morrison[44]	3 days	Morrison[44]	12 days
Pollack[65]	7.5 days	Smith[82]	17 days
Sharpe[66]	4.6 days	Willott & Allard[148]	7.5 days
Perloff & Steinberger[73]	7 days	Silverman[151]	19 days****

* 50 percent positive at seventy-two hours; no exams past seventy-two hours
** "Cervicovaginal" sampling; exact site of sampling not specified
*** 6 percent positive forty-eight hours; no exams past forty-eight hours
**** "Cervicovaginal" scraping; "possibly correct" history

Rupp reviewed the findings in eighty-four cases of alleged sexual assault from the Ft. Lauderdale, Florida, medical examiner's office and noted that no motile sperm were seen more than eight hours after the offense.[67] Wallace-Haagens, et. al., collected daily vaginal fluid samples from twenty-two married women "of proven fertility" and found no motile sperm past twelve hours.[69] Massey, et. al., reviewed the literature in combination with his experience at Philadelphia General Hospital and stated that motile sperm could be seen in the vagina up to six hours postcoitus.[71]

The cervical canal offers an environment to spermatozoa much less hostile than that of the vagina. Cervical mucous is more conducive to the preservation of motility than are vaginal secretions, specially during midcycle (days 14–18).[65] Morrison quotes an anecdotal reference to sperm survival in the cervix at three days after coitus.[44] Pollak describes finding motile sperm in the cervical canal up to seven and a half days after intercourse.[65] He suggests that sperm may not actually be motile *in vivo*, but regain their motility when removed from the cervical mucous and exposed to oxygen. This phenomenon of prolonged spermatozoal survival in cervical mucous may act as a type of storage system just prior to ovulation.[72] Sharpe states that sperm may remain motile for 110 hours (four and six-tenths days) in the cervix but gives no specific data to support this.[66] Perloff and Steinberger studied forty-four "endocrinologically normal, regularly menstruating, and ovulating women" who were artificially inseminated and noted that *in vivo* sperm frequently survive as long as five days and occasionally up to seven days in the cervix.[73] The same authors also describe a phenomenon of aborization of phase lines and phalanges that form when cervical mucous is placed in apposition to seminal fluid. Sperm are quickly trapped in the resultant repositories. This may help explain why there is no existing evidence that sperm once in the cervical canal ever return to the vagina.[29, 66]

From a forensic standpoint two factors concerning sperm in the vagina and cervix deserve emphasis. First, because of the discrepancy in motility between the cervix and vagina, meticulous attention to labeling the origin of collected samples is essential for proper interpretation and estimation of the postcoital interval. Second, motile sperm recovered from the vagina should be interpreted as having survived only in the vagina. Speculation about a "storage" period in the cervix and subsequent return to the vaginal pool, which could thus prolong motility, is without current support.

Morphologic Survival of Spermatozoa

The detection of nonmotile but morphologically intact spermatozoa is usually based upon evaluation of stained smears by the criminalistics laboratory (see table 6–1). Positive findings on the permanent slides will help corroborate the occurrence of a sexual act and, within wider margins than the wet mount, establish the approximate postcoital interval. Davies and Wilson used self-obtained vaginal swabs at known postcoital intervals from female members of their laboratory staff (only four regular couples) and made hematoxylin- and eosin-stained smears to identify sperm.[21] They obtained no negative results before thirty hours and very few negatives up to forty-eight hours; the last positive result occurred at 144 hours (six days). Soules, et. al., used fifteen couples and all samples were positive up to twenty-four hours and 50 percent remained positive at seventy-two hours; no examinations were performed after seventy-two hours.[23] Interestingly, no correlation was found between baseline sperm analysis and duration of morphologic sperm survival after intercourse.

Sperm recovery may also be related to both coital interval and menstrual interval, as well as the anatomic site of the sampling. Morrison examined gram-stained cervical and vaginal smears from 104 patients attending a venereal disease clinic.[44] The longest coital interval that yielded evidence of sperm on the vaginal slide was nine days, with coitus occurring five days after the end of menses. Sharpe does not describe his staining method or present his data, but states that nonmotile sperm are usually found in the vagina seven to twelve hours after coitus.[66] Rupp examined the unstained vaginal aspirates of eighty-four victims of alleged sexual assault and found no evidence of sperm beyond fourteen hours.[67] Wallace-Haagens used daily self-obtained vaginal washings from twenty-two married couples (who recorded coital time) and stained the cellular material with acridine orange.[69] Forty-eight hours after intercourse only 6 percent of slides showed evidence of sperm; no indication or specific notation was made of the longest positive recovery interval.

Silverman and Silverman studied "cervicovaginal" scrapings stained with Papanicolaou stain from 675 women who had volunteered information about the time intervals since their last two episodes of intercourse.[24] Sixty-four percent of the smears obtained the first day after coitus contained spermatozoa. Sperm were seen "irregularly" after seven days and "rarely" after the tenth postcoital day. They also noted no significant difference in the proportion of sperm with and without tails at any postcoital interval and concluded that loss of spermatozoa tails is of no use in estimating the postcoital interval. Other authors have suggested some benefit from quantitating the presence or absence of tails, but these allegations are not well substantiated.[21, 66, 148, 151] The Silverman and Silverman data must be interpreted cautiously in regard to postcoital intervals, because it is not clear as to the exact origin of their samples ("cervicovaginal"). The discrepancy between vaginal and cervical morphologic survival may be just as significant as are the differences in motility.

Less data are available on recovery of stained and/or nonmotile sperm from the cervical canal. Of the 133 cases that Morrison analyzed, he found no positive results from cervical smears examined from the tenth postcoital day onward, with the exception of one smear that showed sperm on the twelfth day after coitus occurring on the eighth day after the end of menses.[44] One of the longest and most frequently quoted intervals for recovery of morphologically intact sperm is seventeen days after intercourse. This reference is from a 1928 edition of a British forensic medicine text.[82] The notation is apparently anecdotal and specifies neither the anatomic site of collection nor specifically whether the spermatozoa were motile or nonmotile. More recently, Silverman broke the record when he reported finding sperm on a Papanicolaou stained cervicovaginal scraping nineteen days after intercourse.[151] He qualified this finding by describing the history as "possibly correct."

Very little information has been published regarding sperm recovery after sodomy or fellatio. The difficulty of interpreting sperm recovered from the rectum because of the potential for contamination from drainage of vaginal contents has already been discussed.[30, 31] Sharpe states that nonmotile sperm have been found in the rectum for periods up to twenty-four hours after the attack.[66] Willott and Allard report that in their experience it is unusual to find tails on spermatozoa recovered from the rectum or anus more than six hours after sodomy.[148] They have found sperm heads up to forty-six hours on an anal swab and sixty-five hours on one rectal swab. Enos and Beyer describe finding oral sperm (also Pap smear stained) up to six hours postassault "despite brushing teeth, using mouthwash, and drinking various fluids."[30] Willott and Allard found sperm on 12 percent of their oral swabs.[148] The longest interval for buccal sperm recovery was six hours and for a specimen from the lips, nine hours.

Acid Phosphatase Analysis

Analysis for acid phosphatase (ACP) in vaginal fluid samples or suspicious stains is routinely performed in sexual assault cases to detect or confirm the presence of semen. The basis for the test is the fact that acid phosphatase activity is five hundred to one thousand times greater in human semen than in any other normal bodily fluid.[26] Unfortunately, the forensic application of this principle is neither simple nor clearcut. Physiological considerations and a variety of methodological and interpretive problems affect the practical usefulness of ACP determinations in the context of rape.

Many Acid Phosphatases

Acid phosphatase is not a single enzyme but an array of many related isoenzymes from a variety of sources. Two main families of ACP are biochemically and genetically distinct. One group has a molecular weight of about fifteen thousand and is cytoplasmic in origin. These ACPs are found in red blood cells and the cytoplasm of many tissues (bone, kidney, placenta, liver, lung, white blood cells). There may be two genetically distinct subclasses within this low molecular weight group.

The other main ACP family comes from lysozymes and has a higher molecular weight of about one hundred thousand. Virtually any tissue that contains lysozymes may produce a high molecular weight ACP. These "tissue" ACPs can be further subdivided into as many as four genetically unique subclasses.

Obviously, differentiating one ACP from the others is a critical issue in the forensic evaluation of rape. Many techniques, including enzyme inhibition, substrate specificity, immunologic cross-reactivity, and electrophoretic behavior, have been employed to distinguish differences between the classes of ACPs. For example, the L-tartrate inhibition test reliably separates the low molecular weight (cytoplasmic) ACPs from the high molecular weight (tissue)

ACPs. This may be important in cases where semen or vaginal fluid samples are mixed with blood.

The two specific acid phosphatases most commonly of interest in the evaluation of sexual assault are both tissue ACPs and are found in semen and vaginal secretions. The seminal ACP originates from the prostate gland. Vaginal secretions from sexually inactive women have been shown to contain low levels of "endogenous" ACP.[22, 25, 26, 43, 75] The exact tissue source of this vaginal ACP is uncertain but has been postulated to be the endometrium.[102] Unfortunately, prostatic and vaginal (endogenous) ACPs, although different in tissue origin, are identical in genetic, immunologic, and biochemical properties. Because a qualitative distinction cannot be made, the only reliable differentiation must be made quantitatively based on the exceptionally high levels of ACP found in prostatic secretions.[146] The problems related to this quantitative evaluation of ACP are discussed in more detail subsequently.

Methodological Considerations

The medical and forensic literature are replete with methodological variations in the collection, analysis, and interpretation of acid phosphatase samples obtained from the vagina (see table 6–2). Most authors use dacron or cotton swabs from the posterior fornix to collect material[21, 22, 23, 26, 28, 29, 43, 74, 76] but some prefer vaginal washings.[25, 75] Methods for storage and transport of specimens also varies from one investigator to another.

A variety of test procedures and substrates have been employed in the ACP assay. Sodium alpha-naphthyl phosphate (ANP) has been used as a substrate in both qualitative and quantitative assessments of ACP activity. The qualitative test combines the ANP with the fluid to be tested; the mixture is briefly incubated and a diazo dye is added. If ACP is present a deep violet color develops. This method appears primarily in the older literature or in combination with other quantitative methods.[25, 28, 67] The current usefulness of qualitative determinations is probably limited to analyzing dried seminal stains.[75] Davies and Wilson semiquantitated the method by recording the amount of time for the color change to begin.[21]

Table 6–2
Comparison of Studies Analyzing Acid Phosphatase Levels in Secretions Collected from the Postcoital Vagina

Author	Substrate	Method	Acid Phosphatase Level			Maximum Time For Seminal ACPP Detection (Hours)
			Endogenous	Equivocal	Seminal	
Duenhoelter[28]	ANP	Qualitative	—	—	—	24
Rupp[67]	ANP	Qualitative	—	—	—	34½
Daves & Wilson[21]	ANP	Semi-Quantitative	>65 sec	30–65 sec 195–	<30 sec	48
Gomez[25]	ANP	Quantitative	<195 U/L	200 U/L	>200U/L	14
	TMP	Quantitative	<50 U/L	50–600U/L	>600 U/L	14
McCloskey[43]	ANP	Quantitative	<25 KAU	—	>25 KAU	48
Masgood[75]	ANP	Quantitative	>50 IU/L	—	<50 IU/L	30
Findley[22]	TMP	Quantitative Autoanalyzer	<100 IU/L	100–300 IU/L	>300IU/L	72
Shumann[29]	TMP	Quantitative Autoanalyzer			>300IU/L	48
Lantz & Eisenberg[74]	TMP	Quantitative Autoanalyzer	<10 U/L	10–50 U/L	>50 U/L	72
Dahlke[76]	TMP	Quantitative Spectrophotometer	<0.5	0.5–1.9	>2.0	36
Soules[23]	TMP	Quantitative Autoanalyzer	<50 U/L	—	>50 U/L	18
Sensabaugh[26, 146]	PNP	Quantitative Spectrophotometer	<6.61*	—	>6.61	92
Allard & Davies[104]	PNP	Quantitative	<20 SU	—	>20 SU	48

Note:
ANP = Alpha-Naphthyl Phosphate   U/L = Units Per Liter
TMP = Thymolphthalein Monophosphate   IU/L = International Units Per Liter
PNP = P-Nitrophenol Phosphate   KAU = King-Armstrong Units
SU = Sigma Units

* Standardized acid phosphatase (SACP) value; 99.0 percent significance level

Quantitative ACP measurements can be done using ANP and recording spectrophotometric absorbances in International Units/liter[25, 75] or King-Armstrong units.[43] This method is very sensitive and may detect very low levels of vaginal (endogenous) ACP.[25, 74] The most commonly employed quantitative method in the literature uses sodium thymolphthalein monophosphate (TMP) as substrate with activity measured spectrophotometrically[23] or on an autoanalyzer.[22, 25, 29] This technique is less sensitive than the ANP method, so the detection threshold is higher and may not pick up low levels of vaginal ACP. Thymolphthalein monophosphate measured values are reported in units/liter. Some authors have used p-nitrophenol phosphate (PNP) as substrate and record spectrophotometic values in International Units/ml of extract.[26, 103, 104]

Even seemingly subtle differences in handling or analysis of evidence material may have a significant effect on the results and conclusions of a given study. The issue compounds when attempting to compare the work of different investigators. Familiarity with the local method; its advantages, and limitations provides a helpful perspective from which to evaluate the forensic ACP data from a specific case.

Quantitative Considerations

When the crime lab analysis of vaginal swabs detects a high molecular weight ACP, the next task will logically be to determine the tissue of origin. Since endogenous and prostatic ACPs are qualitatively identical, the decision must be based on the amount of acid phosphatase recovered. The finding of "significantly" elevated ACP in the vaginal pool is considered reliable proof of the presence of semen and recent sexual contact.[21, 22, 23, 25, 28, 29, 43, 68, 70, 75]

The challenge for the criminalist is to set a threshold value that reliably proves seminal origin when a specified level is exceeded. Many variables complicate this endeavor. Considerable endogenous variations have been reported between individuals, as well as fluctuations of a single individual's baseline.[22, 25, 26] Baseline levels may also vary in relation to the menstrual cycle, but the practical significance of this remains controversial.[26, 74]

Not only do endogenous levels of ACP vary over time, but so do the values of seminal ACP after deposition in the vagina. It is clear that prostatic ACP activity in the postcoital vagina declines after intercourse but the rate of decline is extremely variable.[21, 22, 26, 43] Sensabaugh studied the fate of ACP in the postcoital vagina and concluded that decay occurs in three phases.[26, 146] The first phase shows immediate and rapid decline of activity. This pattern suggests a response to a physical process (probably drainage of seminal constituents from the vagina). Phase two shows marked variability in the rate of decline and probably represents a combination of continued mechanical drainage (from upright body position) and dilution from vaginal secretions. Approximately ten to twelve hours after intercourse the third phase begins and is characterized by a slower rate of decline over the next forty-eight to sixty hours until baseline (endogenous) levels are reached. Although initially considered, there is now no solid evidence to support the idea that enzymatic decay plays any role in the decline of ACP activity in the postcoital vagina.[150]

When the broad spectrum of individual variation in endogenous vaginal and seminal ACP activity is coupled with laboratory procedural differences, there is little wonder about the lack of agreement in the literature regarding threshold values for differentiating endogenous from seminal ACP. Table 6–2 summarizes a number of studies that have evaluated postcoital acid phosphatase. Once again, local crime lab standards and data base must be relied upon to make a rational judgment about the ACP level in a given case.

An important corollary issue to postcoital ACP decline is the determination of the postcoital interval. Unfortunately, the loss of prostatic ACP activity after intercourse occurs with wider variation than the decline of sperm motility and is subject to numerous methodologic variables. Despite these limitations, several authors have generated ACP decay curves based on varying techniques. Findley constructed an ACP decay curve with four time categories of probable postcoital intervals from one to seventy-two hours.[22] Lantz and Eisenberg derived a logarithmic ACP curve with levels reaching baseline (10 U/L) at ninety-six hours and threshold (50 U/L) at seventy-two hours.[74] Allard and Davies formulated an ACP decay curve with no positive findings more than forty-eight hours postintercourse and very few positives in the thirty-seven-to-forty-eight-hour interval.[104]

Sensabaugh used p-nitrophenyl phosphate as substrate and measured the results spectrophotometrically.[26] He combined his data with that of other authors (who used a variety of other test procedures) by factoring out unit and scale differences to arrive at a unitless standardized acid phosphatase (SACP) value for each piece of data. With this expanded data base the author was able to apply a more definitive statistical analysis. He looked at the range of endogenous ACP levels and postcoital ACP values and determined the probabilities of overlap (false positives and false negatives) depending on where the threshold confidence level is set. In subsequent work, Sensabaugh and his colleagues have concluded that postcoital swab values begin to fall below endogenous threshold levels (99 percent confidence interval) beginning as early as three to six hours after intercourse. By twelve to fifteen hours postcoitus, 50 percent of swab values fall below the threshold.[146]

Potential Interferences and Interpretive Considerations

A number of factors may contribute to the risk of false positive interpretations (see figure 6–5). Various substances, which could be

False Positives
    Methodological variables
    Endogenous vaginal acid phosphatase above threshold values
    Contaminants
    Pregnancy
    Bacterial vaginitis
    Recent use of feminine hygeine products

False Negatives
    Methodological variables
    Any factor that limits detection or recovery of seminal constituents (figure 6–2)
    Elevated temperature:
        Storage or transport of specimens
        Febrile victim
    Prostatic disease (for example, chronic prostatitis) in assailant

Figure 6–5. *Potential Interferences with Acid Phosphatase Determinations in the Forensic Evaluation of the Sexually Assaulted Adult Female*

potential contaminants, have been shown to react chemically in ways that may simulate positive results in acid phosphatase determinations. The potential for any given contaminant to produce a false positive will depend on the specific ACP analysis employed. In general, contamination-generated false positives are more of a problem in the evaluation of stains than they are in material collected from the vagina.[150] The list of contaminants includes certain vegetable extracts (particularly cauliflower juice), gorse seed extracts, and household bleach.[21, 22, 70]

The vaginal milieu may also influence the ACP determination, as demonstrated by reports of increased activity in the vaginas of some pregnant women and in samples taken from women with large numbers of vaginal bacteria.[21, 25, 75] Some feminine hygiene products may contain phenols and/or naphthols that can react with the diazo dyes used in qualitative ACP determinations and thus be falsely interpreted as positive.[177]

The issue of false negative ACP determination also limits the usefulness of the assay. Just as with the evaluation of spermatozoa, the effects of drainage in the ambulatory victim and dilution (from menstrual flow, admixing with vaginal secretions or douching) may significantly decrease the amount of ACP available for analysis and thus lower the measured value. Some investigators have postulated that high vaginal pH may enhance the degradation of ACP but the data is anecdotal.[22, 25, 150]

As the temperature rises, acid phosphatase becomes progressively more unstable with resultant rapid loss of activity.[22, 25, 26] Fever in the victim may increase the rate at which ACP activity is lost.[70] Improper storage conditions (such as inadequate drying or elevated ambient temperature) may also adversely affect the measured result. Adequate drying of swabs (sixty minutes in a stream of cool, dry air) is essential, because the degree of moisture in the sample greatly influences the amount of ACP recovered.[26, 146]

If the assailant wears a condom or fails to ejaculate, obviously no ACP will be found. The limits of normal variation in acid phosphatase activity in semen from different individuals are quite broad.[22, 29] Prostatic disease, primarily chronic prostatitis, may yield an ejaculate with markedly low levels of ACP.[101] Although somewhat controversial, there are probably no significant differ-

ences in seminal ACP activity between the ejaculates of vasectomized and nonvasectomized men.[74, 105]

Several reports have been published in which spermatozoa were
found postcoitally but the laboratory failed to detect elevated ACP
levels.[8, 28, 107, 129] Discounting methodological error, the most
likely explanation is the fact that tests for sperm in the postcoital
vagina are both more sensitive and more specific than are ACP
assays. Dilution from endogenous secretions decreases the recovery
of both sperm and ACP, but sperm are relatively easier to find after
dilution. The issue of vaginal background levels of ACP and varying
criteria for threshold values to confirm the presence of seminal
ACP, coupled with the broad spectrum of reported ACP decay
rates, undoubtedly contributes to the problem.

The acid phosphatase determination is probably most helpful
forensically when no sperm are found on the wet mount or
permanent slides but ACP levels are elevated to a degree consistent
with the presence of seminal constituents.[8, 14, 25, 27, 28, 29, 67, 78] As
discussed previously, many factors may contribute to this scenario,
including impaired spermatogenesis, depleted stores, or impaired
sperm delivery (see figure 6–3).

The presence of acid phosphatase in sexual assault case material
may be a helpful adjunct in corroborating the occurrence of a recent
sexual act. A positive finding, however, must be scrutinized in the
context of a number of caveats. Physiologic, temporal, quantitative,
and methodologic variables may all affect measured values and thus
influence interpretation. The validity of any determination of
postcoital interval or affirmation of seminal constituents based on
acid phosphatase analysis must rely on the data base and experience
of the individual laboratory performing and interpreting the test.[23]
If ACP values are reliably above the local threshold to prove
seminal origin, a recent sexual act can be inferred. The converse is
not true. Negative findings disprove neither sexual contact nor rape.

p30

The continuing search for other semen-specific markers has yielded
some promising findings. An ideal marker should be biologically

specific (that is, found only in the male reproductive tract), independent of the presence or absence of sperm, stable in seminal stains and within the vaginal milieu, and be detectable at trace levels. In 1978, Sensabaugh isolated and described p30, a glycoprotein of seminal origin with a molecular weight of about thirty-thousand daltons.[106] This same substance has been independently characterized by a number of other investigators and labeled gamma-seminoprotein, semen E_1 antigen, and prostate-specific antigen.[149, 179] Watt, et al., have recently sequenced this substance and found it to be a single polypeptide chain of 240 amino acid residues.[179] The primary structure shows a high degree of sequence homology with other serine proteases of the kallikrein family.

The p30 antigen is derived from the prostate epithelial cells and found in seminal plasma and male urine. Most prostatic neoplasms and their metastases may produce high levels of this antigen, making it valuable in tumor detection and monitoring. No significant quantitative differences were found when semen from vasectomized men was compared with samples from nonvasectomized men.[149] To date, p30 has not been found in any female tissue or bodily secretion.

In the forensic investigation of sexual assault, p30 offers two important advantages over acid phosphatase as a semen marker. First, p30 is unique to the male genitourinary tract; there is no problem with vaginal background activity (as there is with ACP). The finding of any p30 in the evidence material confirms the presence of semen. A positive p30 test reliably identifies semen regardless of whether ACP is elevated or sperm are found. In a recent study, Graves, Sensabaugh, and Blake describe a simple and economical enzyme-linked immunosorbent assay (ELISA) for p30.[149] They analyzed vaginal swabs from twenty-seven alleged sexual assault victims in whom no acid phosphatase was detected. In seven cases, p30 was found. One victim had a positive p30 despite the absence of spermatozoa.

The second advantage follows from the first and relies on the predictable loss of p30 activity over time. As discussed in the preceding section, the decline of measured acid phosphatase activity in the postcoital vagina is extremely variable; some samples reach endogenous threshold levels within three hours after intercourse, while others remain above the cutoff point for as long as sixty to ninety-two hours.[146] When plotted on a log scale, p30 activity is lost in an approximately linear fashion. This decline occurs at about the same rate as with acid phosphatase, but because there is no vaginal background, the p30 curve can be reliable followed over a longer interval. The mean time to reach the lower limits of the vaginal detection threshold is twenty-seven hours, with the range from thirteen to forty-seven hours.[149] Thus, p30 provides an additional point of reference with which to estimate the postcoital interval. It follows that a positive p30 finding functionally sets the upper limit for the postcoital interval at about forty-eight hours.

The discovery and elucidation of p30 provides a helpful adjunct in the search for objective evidence of recent sexual contact in cases of alleged sexual assault. Methodological simplification has made p30 evaluation a routine procedure in the analysis of rape evidence material.

Genetic Profiling

The typing of genetic markers in the forensic evaluation of sexual assault has received considerable attention in recent years. Ideally, enough sample material can be collected from the victim, from traces left by the assailant, and from the possible suspect(s), to develop and compare genetic profiles of the individuals potentially involved in the event. Although standard genetic profiling is not as uniquely specific as fingerprints, it can greatly narrow the suspect population. The more definitive the genetic typing, the greater the probability of excluding false suspects and the more restricted the true suspect group.

Many markers have been studied for use in the forensic investigation of sexual assault.[45, 46, 110, 111, 112, 146, 154, 155, 156] In practical application, only three are commonly found in semen in adequate amounts for routine typing. These are the ABO blood group antigens and the two enzyme markers Peptidase A (Pep A) and Phosphoglucomutase (PGM). Each of these markers may also be detected in low levels in vaginal secretions. As in the ACP determination, this problem of "vaginal background" necessitates the differentiation of substances that could have originated from the victim from those that can be confidently classified as foreign (deposited by the assailant). The investigation is facilitated by the fact that these genetically determined markers are expressed in blood. Reference typing of the individuals involved requires only a blood sample, not semen or vaginal secretions.

Blood Group Typing

The human red cell membrane contains hundreds of genetically determined antigens. Any well-defined system of RBC antigens controlled by a locus having a variable number of allelic genes is termed a blood group. More than twenty such groups have been characterized. The best studied and most important forensically is the ABO group. Closely associated with the ABO system is another antigen called "H," which is the precursor of A and B antigens. Although the H and ABO loci are not genetically linked, their functional relationship has prompted the convention of treating these antigens as a single system with the notation ABO(H).

Most RBC antigens are bound to the cell membrane, while others (including ABO(H) antigens) are soluble. Soluble antigens may be secreted into other bodily fluids (saliva, semen, sweat, vaginal secretions, and so on). This characteristic is controlled by a pair of allelic genes, Se and se, with Se being dominant, so that individuals homozygous (SeSe) or heterozygous (Sese) for the Se gene are "secretors." About 80 percent of the population are secretors, with a 20 percent homozygous (sese) nonsecretors. Secretor status is usually assessed by determining ABO type from a blood sample and analyzing a saliva sample (from a chewed, air-dried gauze pad) for the presence of the same ABO(H) antigens. Results can be confirmed by typing RBCs for Lewis antigens (Lewis^a = secretor, Lewis^b = nonsecretor).

Cell bound antigens (for example, vaginal epithelial cells or microorganisms) can create interference during the analysis of soluble antigens from evidence material. Therefore, soluble ABO(H) antigen testing is best carried out using cell free extracts. The preferred method uses a semiquantitative agglutination inhibition test that is read microscopically.[146]

A number of factors must be considered to properly interpret the results of ABO(H) marker testing. First, the victim's ABO type and secretor status must be ascertained to provide a clear picture of the type and distribution of the expected native antigens. After the victim's marker pattern has been established the next step is the analysis of the evidence material for antigens qualitatively different from the victim's. If other than the expected markers are found, these "foreign" antigens can be inferred to have originated from the assailant and secreted into his semen. For example, a secretor positive, blood type O victim is expected to have only H antigen in her vaginal secretions; if A antigen was found it can be reasonably argued that the victim had recent sexual contact with a secretor positive, blood type A individual (see table 6–3).

In addition to the qualitative analysis of expected and foreign antigens, quantitative factors may play a significant role in the interpretation of blood group evidence. If spermatozoa have been detected on the permanent slides, a determination of sperm density (usually reported as $1+$ to $4+$) offers a rough estimate of the amount of semen deposited. The presence of foreign antigens can be corroborated if their measured amount is proportional to the estimated semen content. If no foreign antigens are found, but expected antigens are recovered in amounts greatly in excess of those anticipated from normal vaginal secretions and the estimate

Table 6–3

ABO Blood Types and Antigens in the Forensic Evaluation of Sexual Assault

Victim's ABO Phenotype	Expected Antigens (from victim)	Foreign Antigens (presumed from assailant's semen)
0	H	A B
A	A H	B
B	B H	A
AB	A B H	—

of semen content is high, then it may be inferred that the victim and assailant share the same ABO blood type. If the semen content is high but only normal levels of expected antigens are found, the assailant may be a nonsecretor. When both sperm and foreign antigens are absent, the determination of antigen source must be based solely on the amount recovered. Obviously, the fewer pieces of data available for comparison and confirmation the greater the level of uncertainty becomes.

Other factors may also contribute to inconclusive ABO(H) antigen testing (see figure 6–6). Insufficient quantities of evidence material, whether from condom use, ejaculatory failure, drainage, dilution from endogenous secretions, or glycolytic degradation, is a recurrent problem in the forensic evaluation of rape. Other familiar issues are vaginal background activity and contamination. Davies and Wilson have concluded that blood group antigens were only detected at useful levels if collected within forty-eight hours of intercourse.[21]

Since soluble ABO(H) antigens are not present in nonsecretor's bodily fluids, evaluating this 20 percent of the population is more difficult. One approach that may be helpful under certain circumstances is to analyze the cellular debris found in evidence material. This debris may include sperm or epithelial cells from the assailant that contain membrane-bound ABO(H) antigens that are not mediated by secretor status.

Enzyme and Protein Markers

Phosphoglucomutase (PGM) and Peptidase A (Pep A), the two enzyme markers commonly used in genetic profiling, are found in

Any factor that limits detection or recovery of seminal constituents in general (figure 6–2)
Nonsecretor assailant
Victim and assailant with same blood type or other shared antigens
Quantity of material collected insufficient for reliable analysis
Vaginal background activity or contamination
Assault/evidence collection interval over forty-eight hours
Variations in testing methodology

Figure 6–6. *Factors Limiting the Usefulness of Blood Group Antigen Testing in the Forensic Evaluation of Sexual Assault*

semen and vaginal secretions regardless of ABO blood type or secretor status. Both are analyzed electrophoretically and both have three main phenotypes (1, 2-1, and 2). PGM is polymorphic in all populations and has been extensively studied as a genetic marker in blood and seminal stains. Isoelectric focusing and low pH electrophesis has made it possible to divide PGM beyond its three phenotypes into ten genetically distinct subtypes. Peptidase A, although present in semen in relatively high amounts, is only polymorphic in the black population, so its forensic application is limited to cases in which the perpetrator was thought to be black.

The measurable activity of both PGM and Pep A in the postcoital vagina declines rapidly. PGM samples obtained more than six hours after coitus are seldom helpful and Pep A probably doesn't survive past three hours in the vagina.[146] Furthermore, improperly preserved (inadequately dried) specimens will reduce the likelihood of obtaining meaningful results. Seminal stains from the patient's body, from her clothing, or from the crime scene frequently provide the criminalist with more material that is less contaminated than vaginal samples.

In secretors, saliva may contain the gamut of soluble antigens, enzymes, and proteins. When properly collected and preserved this information may facilitate the overall development of a genetic profile. Because oral contact (kissing, biting, fellatio, cunnilingus) or the use of saliva as a lubricant is common in sexual assault (up to 30 percent of cases[176]), the history should specifically explore these possibilities and the exam and evidence collection should be directed accordingly.

A caveat about the interpretation of PGM data in this context should be emphasized. Evidence material that contains mixtures of saliva and semen present a special challenge to the forensic analyst. Sensabaugh and colleagues showed that seminal PGM_1 isoenzyme patterns are substantially altered in semen contaminated by saliva, with the extent of alteration dependent on the amount of saliva in the sample.[176] The biochemistry of this phenomenon is incompletely understood but the isoenzyme conversion pattern from type to type is predictable. Strict adherence to the guidelines for interpretation (as outlined by Price, et al.[78]) probably offer the best hedge against error.[176] Subsequent research has shown that the

PGM pattern shift in semen-saliva mixtures can be reversed by the addition of a substantial reducing agent.[150]

Various proteins and enzymes in plasma and from red blood cells have been shown to be genetically polymorphic. Considerable research effort has helped demonstrate the presence of many of these substances in vaginal secretions and semen.[45, 46, 155] The typing capability and practical use of any given marker depends primarily on quantitative considerations. These factors include the amount of marker initially present, the stability of the marker in the evidence material, the dilution in the stain or swab extract, the presence of interfering contaminants, and the detection threshold of the assay procedure. Other markers, while present in adequate amounts, have limited forensic application because their polymorphism (and hence their discrimination potential) is restricted. Figure 6–7 lists some of the genetic markers that have been investigated but are only clinically useful under the most ideal of circumstances.

Practical Applications Of Genetic Profiling

The objective of the genetic analysis of evidence material is to determine the probability of whether a given individual could have

Phosphoglucose Isomerase (PGI)
Amylase
Transferrin (TF)
Adenylate Kinase (AK)
Esterase D (Es-D)
Glucose-6-Phosphate Dehydrogenase (G-6-PD)
6-Phosphogluconase Dehydrogenase (6-PDG)
Carbonic Anhydrase-II (CA-II)
Glyoxalase-I (GLO-1)
Adenosine Deaminase (ADA)
Alpha$_1$—Antitrypsin
Haptoglobin (Hp)
Immunoglobin Gm (IgG)
Immunoglobin Inv (IgG + IgA)
Group Specific Component (GC)
Sperm Diaphorase

Figure 6–7. *Genetic Markers in Semen that are Rarely of Practical Use in the Evaluation of Sexual Assault*[46]

been the source of the sample. To accomplish this in a sexual assault investigation, three genetic profiles (one from the victim, one from the evidence material, and one from the potential suspect) must be generated and compared. Markers recovered from the evidence that are qualitatively or quantitatively different from the victim's pattern are presumed to have been deposited by the assailant. Any foreign antigens or enzymes found in the evidence material must then be compared with the genetic marker pattern from the potential suspect. If the patterns are different that particular suspect can be excluded. If the patterns are the same the laboratory must determine the percentage of the general population that also share this specific genetic profile.

Routine typing relies on four markers: secretor status, ABO blood type, PGM, and Pep A. Under extraordinary circumstances additional markers (see figure 6–7) may come into play. Each marker is inherited independently of the others and the types and subtypes of these markers occur in the population in known frequencies (which vary somewhat from race to race). To calculate the frequency of a given genetic pattern in the population is a simple matter of multiplying the percentages of occurrence of each individual marker.

For example, consider an individual who is a secretor (80 percent in the caucasian population), blood type O (45 percent in the caucasian population) and PGM subtype $2+, 1+$ (25 percent in the caucasian population). The frequency of this combination of types is 80 percent $\times$ 45 percent $\times$ 25 percent = 9 percent. In other words, 9 percent of the caucasian population has this pattern. As the frequencies of individual markers decrease or the number of markers used increases, the discrimination potential of the analysis improves. In the preceding example, simply changing the blood type to AB (4 percent of the population) decreases the suspect population to only 0.8 percent (80 percent $\times$ 4 percent $\times$ 25 percent = 0.8 percent).

The emerging technology of genetic engineering has recently yielded some spinoffs that may revolutionize genetic typing in forensic science. The DNA sequence in the human genome is unique to the individual. Differences in deoxyribonucleic acid sequence between individuals can be detected as size polymorphisms in restriction endonuclease digested DNA. Because these polymorphisms are inherited as Mendelian traits, they may be reliably used in genetic studies.[174, 175]

High molecular mass DNA can be isolated from the nuclei of sperm recovered from evidence material. This DNA can then be analyzed for restriction fragment length polymorphisms (RFLPs). What results is an electrophoretic "DNA fingerprint" of the donor. The probability of differentiating two individuals based on their specific DNA patterns approaches certainty.[174] The use of this technique in the forensic evaluation of rape is still currently in the realm of research, but the potential is staggering. As methodology is refined and clinical experience with actual case material accumulates, it may become possible to conclusively and reliably identify or exclude a sexual assault suspect from the DNA fingerprints extracted from the physical evidence.

Hair Analysis and Fingernail Scrapings

Nearly every evidentiary exam protocol calls for pubic hair combings, pubic and head hair reference samples, and fingernail scrapings from the victim. Little has been published regarding the ultimate usefulness of these endeavors. A struggling victim may scratch the assailant and collect cells and blood from her attacker under her fingernails. Sufficient material may be removed to permit a detailed forensic evaluation for genetic markers and thus be quite helpful in suspect elimination or inclusion.

The usefulness of hair analysis is more questionable. The analytical matching of hairs is both "art" and "science."[113] A detailed hair comparison takes about six hours and requires twelve to fifteen hairs obtained from random locations on the victim to cover the range of potential variation.[23] If possible, the control hairs should be plucked rather than clipped, since the roots contribute three additional morphologic characteristics and, potentially, genetic material. The usefulness of forensic hair analysis is based on the concept that individuality stems from a persistent microscopic pattern of structural components. The experience and expertise of the examiner is critically important in the interpretation and validity of results. Biochemical analysis is technically more problematic but functionally more objective and therefore more reliable.

There are three facets of the hair analysis. First, the pubic combings are examined and compared with the reference hairs of the victim and a decision is made as to whether any "foreign" material has been detected. Foreign material could include animal hairs, synthetic fibers, or human hair that is morphologically distinct from those of the victim. The second phase requires examination and hair sampling from the suspect to search for positive structural comparisons that may confirm contact with the victim.

The third component of the hair analysis is biochemical. Hair is basically dead protein but the hair bulb and root sheath may contain enough viable cells for genetic typing.[155] Recent research has demonstrated the potential for DNA typing from single hairs.[197] Plucking the reference hairs from the victim provides an important baseline if genetic studies on root material are employed. A positive comparison only indicates contact, not rape. A negative result proves nothing, because the incidence of hair exchange during rape is probably quite low. Soules, et al., studied fifteen couples after voluntary intercourse but failed to document hair exchange in a single case.[23] Sternbaugh also found pubic hair sampling to be unproductive.[18]

Conclusion

In some ways, forensic science is similar to archaeology. The archaeologist studies the artifacts and debris left by a past culture to understand how its people lived and related to their world. The forensic team (police investigator, examining nurse, physician, and crimimalist) must work together to collect and analyze physical evidence—traces left after the crime—to reconstruct the event in question. This forensic reconstruction often provides reliable and independent corroboration of the history, which allows much of the investigation to proceed irrespective of victim involvement. The victim's burden is lighter because the forensic investigators share the responsibility for describing the crime. From the district attorney's standpoint, a much stronger case can be built if it is supported by objective and scientific data, not just the testimony of the victim.

When the health care provider performs an evidentiary exam on a sexual assault victim, he or she becomes part of the criminal justice system. To insure maximum yield from the exam, a high level of consciousness about several points must be maintained. Strict adherence to chain of evidence procedures is mandatory. Faithful compliance to local protocols for evidence collection and specimen preservation cannot be overstressed. In view of the often vast interlaboratory differences in methodology and interpretation of many assays, forensic conclusions should only be drawn from the experience and data base of the criminalistics department performing the analyses. With proper training and appropriate attention to detail, the medical examiner plays an essential role in facilitating justice.

7
Treatment Considerations

The treatment needs of the sexual assault victim are both curative and preventative. The curative aspects center around the acute medical and emotional trauma sustained as a direct result of the attack. Obviously, acute injuries in the rape victim are handled in the same expeditious fashion as they would be in any other emergency patient. The risks of venereal disease and unwanted pregnancy developing as a consequence of the rape must be thoroughly and candidly discussed with the victim. The decision whether to begin prophylactic therapy immediately or to defer treatment pending reevaluation at the time of the followup visit should be made by the victim after consultation with the medical examiner. The victim must understand the potential risks and benefits of treatment in the context of her individual circumstances.

Risk of Pregnancy

Estimating the realistic chance of a pregnancy resulting from a single unprotected intercourse is difficult because so many variables are involved. The fecundity of victim and assailant are often unknown. Any factor that limits or prevents the deposition of spermatozoa in the victim's vagina will obviously change the risk of impregnation (see figures 6–2 and 6–3). The time the act occurs in the victim's menstrual cycle and the resultant proximity to ovulation is a critical issue. Tietze assumed that fertile coitus was only possible for a twelve-to-twenty-four-hour period per cycle and statistically analyzed the probability of pregnancy without regard to time in the menstrual cycle.[95] He concluded that the overall risk of pregnancy from a single unprotected coitus was between 2 percent and 4 percent.

Many authors have studied the probability of conception as related to coital timing and ovulation (see table 7–1).[100, 108, 109] In a woman with regular menstrual cycles, the time of ovulation can usually be ascertained by using basal body temperatures (BBT). The acute temperature rise (usually at or near midcycle) occurs during ovulation.[109] The day of the temperature shift is usually designated as day 0 with preovulatory days counted as minus (−1, −2) and postovulatory days as (+1, +2). The greatest likelihood of conception occurs when sperm are deposited between day −6 and day +1.[100, 108, 109] Schwartz, et al.,[100] investigated 821 cycles in couples who underwent one controlled intracervical insemination per cycle and found the highest conception rates on days −1 (21 percent) and −3 (20 percent).[100] Barrett and Marshall followed 241 couples using BBT for fertility awareness and applied quantal regression to analyze their data.[108] They estimated the maximum probability of conception to be 30 percent on day −2. Vollman reviewed the literature on natural family planning and concluded that the highest risk of pregnancy occurred on day −1 (22 percent) and day −3 (20 percent).[109]

It is reasonable to assume these percentages represent the maximum probabilities of conception, because the research populations were by and large motivated, compliant married couples of proven or likely fecundity. A great deal of baseline data (semen analyses, BBTs, etc.) were amassed on most couples before inclusion in the studies. Clearly, there are many more unknowns involved in a single act of coitus that occurs during a sexual assault. The utility

Table 7–1
Risk of Pregnancy (%) from Unprotected Intercourse

Cycle day	−6	−5	−4	−3	−2	−1	ovulation	+1	+2
Schwartz et al[100]			8	20	13	21	15	11	9
Barrett & Marshall[108]		13	20	17	30	14		7	
Vollman[109]	10	10	11	20	15	22		6	0

Note: Overall average 2%–4% during entire cycle
Source: Tietz[95]

of the previous statistics lies in their use as a guideline for helping the rape victim assess her maximum risk of an unwanted pregnancy and assisting her in deciding whether to begin a postcoital interceptive method.

Interceptive Methods

If the patient deems the risk of unwanted pregnancy to be unacceptably high, the clinician should be prepared to discuss the available alternatives for postcoital interception. The choices are basically two: hormonal intervention or the insertion of an intrauterine device (usually copper-containing). Both methods are "interceptives" that prevent pregnancy by interfering with implantation. Interceptives are neither contraceptives nor abortifacients since they do not inhibit fertilization nor disrupt an already implanted pregnancy.[90]

The physiology and biochemistry of postcoital interception is complex and incompletely understood. Normally, the ovum remains in the fallopian tube for two or three days after ovulation and is slowly propelled toward the uterine cavity by muscular peristalsis and the beating action of luminal cilia. Sphincters at the ampullary-isthmic junction (AIJ) and uterotubular junction (UTJ) probably influence the tubular transport time. The delay in tubal migration of the ovum allows fertilization to occur in the oviduct and is essential for synchronization of egg development and uterine receptivity.[90] An intact, functioning corpus luteum is necessary to insure the integrity of an early pregnancy.[90, 92] The delicate interrelationships among hypothalmus, pituitary, ovary, fallopian tube, and uterus are vulnerable to disruption at a number of sites.

Estrogen Interceptives

Many drugs have been employed as postcoital agents, but by far the best investigated and most widely used are the estrogens. Their mechanism of action in preventing pregnancy is multifactorial. Alteration of zygote transport is significant and dose-related. Small doses of estrogen cause acceleration of egg transport and premature expulsion of the ova into the unreceptive endometrial cavity.[90, 92] Increased ciliary action and enhanced uterine-directed flow of oviduct fluid are probably the contributory estrogen stimulated events.[92] Larger doses of estrogen (in the range of common clinical usage) slow tubular transport and create "tubal locking," probably by causing increased tone in the AIJ and UTJ sphincters.[90, 92, 97, 114] Although still somewhat speculative, there is some evidence that estrogens may have a direct cytotoxic effect on the ovum.[90, 92] In view of the mechanisms of action, it is technically more accurate to refer to the interceptive effects of estrogen as postovulatory rather than postcoital.

A wide variety of estrogen compounds (natural, synthetic, and conjugated) in different dosage schedules have been investigated as potential postovulatory interceptives. There has been surprisingly close agreement among many investigators on the qualifications for participation in postovulatory estrogen studies (see figure 7–1). The patient must be free of any of the absolute contraindications to oral contraceptive use (known or suspected carcinoma of the breast, known or suspected estrogen dependent neoplasia, undiagnosed abnormal genital bleeding, known or suspected preexisting pregnancy, current or past thrombophlebitis or thromboembolic disorder, cerebrovascular or coronary artery disease, benign or malignant hepatic neoplasia).[87] Most authors agree that to be effective therapy must be started within seventy-two hours of exposure.[4, 87, 92, 93, 99, 116] Ideally, hormonal therapy should be initiated within twenty-four hours of the unprotected coitus.

In an effort to reduce operant variables, most investigators have limited eligibility in postovulatory estrogen studies to women who

Known or suspected carcinoma of the breast
Known or suspected estrogen dependent neoplasia
Undiagnosed abnormal genital bleeding
Known or suspected preexisting pregnancy
Current or past thrombophlebitis or thromboembolic disorder
Cerebrovascular or coronary artery disease
Benign or malignant hepatic neoplasia

Figure 7–1. *Contraindications to Postovulatory Contraception with Estogens*

are within seventy-two hours of the unprotected exposure and excluded women who have had other episodes of unprotected intercourse in the current cycle. These exclusions are methodologically appropriate in a research context but may be unreasonable in the clinical setting of sexual assault. The data clearly confirm that when these two restrictions are waived the statistical effectiveness of hormonal interceptives declines. However, given the lack of serious side effects with these methods, a potential for decreased efficacy seems insufficient justification to withhold therapy from a rape victim who presents more than seventy-two hours after the assault or who has had unprotected consensual coitus in the same cycle. Postovulatory hormonal interception should still be available to these women, but they should fully understand and acknowledge the augmented risk of method failure created by special circumstances.

There is also good consensus that the decision about whether to undergo treatment must be made by the patient, and, if treatment is chosen, then written, informed consent is prudent.[4, 87, 93, 94] A written information sheet describing the method of action, the risks, and side effects is generally given to each patient. The importance of followup and alternatives in the case of a method failure should also be included in the patient education material.

Diethylstilbestrol

For years, diethylstilbestrol (DES) has probably been the most commonly prescribed "morning after" treatment. Haspels gave DES postcoitally to 545 women in doses from 25mg to 50mg daily for five days after unprotected coitus.[96] Four pregnancies (rate = 0.7 percent) occurred in this group (see table 7–2). In one of these four cases, other unprotected episodes of intercourse were known to have occurred in the same cycle and the remaining three pregnancies were in women given 30mg (or less) of DES daily. No pregnancies occurred in women given 50mg daily (25mg BID for five days). Kuchera gave 1,410 women DES at a dose of 25mg BID for five days following unprotected intercourse.[93, 94] There were no pregnancies in the 1,217 women who met study criteria and

Table 7–2

Comparison of Method Failure Rates (Pregnancies) after Postovulatory Interception Employing Diethylstilbestrol (DES), Ethinylestradiol (EE), or Conjugated Estrogens (CE)

Author	Drug	Dosage Regime	Number of Women	Number of Pregnancies	Pregnancy Rate
Haspels[96]	DES	25–50mg PO Daily × 5 days	545	4*	0.7 %
Kuchera[93, 94]	DES	50mg PO Daily × 5 days	1217	0	0
Haspels[96]	EE	1–5mg PO Daily × 5 days	2336	13**	0.6 %
Dixon, et al[87]	EE	5mg PO Daily × 5 days	546	4	0.7 %
Lehfeldt[98]	EE	6–25mg PO Total over 3–5 days	133	1***	0.75%
Dixon, et al[87]	CE	30mg PO Daily × 5 days	430	7	1.62%
Notelvitz & Bard[116]	CE	30mg PO Daily × 5 days	359	1	0.3 %
Crist[92]	CE	30mg PO Daily × 5 days	194	0	0
Yussman[92]	CE	50mg IV Daily × 2 doses	200	0	0

* One pregnancy occurred in a woman with other episodes of unprotected coitus in the study cycle; and three other pregnancies were in women given 30mg (or less) of DES daily

** Only two pregnancies occurred in women given 5mg EE daily for five days

*** Exposure-treatment interval = eight days

complied with followup. Six pregnancies occurred in the group who could not be included in the study group because of multiple episodes of unprotected coitus in the study cycle (all six) and initiation of treatment more than seventy-two hours after intercourse (2/6). Despite a high incidence of side effects (discussed later) the proven efficacy of 25mg of DES twice daily for five days made this regime the most commonly employed postovulatory treatment and the yardstick by which other methods are judged.

Ethinylestradiol

Another synthetic estrogen, ethinylestradiol (EE), had also been widely studied and used as a postovulatory interceptive. In addition to using DES, Haspels also used EE in dosages from 1–5mg daily for five days in 2,336 women in need of an interceptive.[96] Thirteen pregnancies occurred in the EE treated group for an overall failure rate of 0.6 percent. Only two pregnancies developed in women receiving the 5mg dose of EE. The other intraceptive failures were attributed to inadequate dosage, delay in initiation of treatment, and/or other unprotected exposures within the same cycle. In a four-year, multicenter study, Dixon, et al., prescribed EE (5mg daily for five days) to 546 women who were within seventy-two hours of a single unprotected episode of coitus.[87] Four pregnancies resulted (rate = 0.7 percent); apparently all four can be considered method failures. Lehfeldt reported his experience in 133 patients using small doses of EE (6 to 10mg total dose over three days) for some women while others received a more standard dose of 5mg daily for five days. Only one pregnancy occurred and that was in a woman who delayed treatment until eight days after exposure.[98]

Conjugated Estrogens

Conjugated equine estrogens (CE) have been studied as postovulatory interceptives but there is less experience with these agents than with diethylstilbestrol or ethinylestradiol. As part of their study, Dixon and associates administered conjugated estrogens (30mg daily for five days) to 340 women within seventy-two hours of a single unprotected intercourse.[87] Seven pregnancies resulted in this group (rate = 1.62). Notelovitz and Bard also used 30mg of conjugated estrogen daily for five days in 359 women who requested an interceptive.[116] Their qualifications for inclusion in the study were very similar to those required by Dixon, et al.[87] Only one of the 359 patients became pregnant (rate = 0.3 percent). Crist used the same criteria and dosage for 194 women and had no pregnancies.[92] Yussman employed 50mg per day of conjugated equine estrogens given intravenously for two consecutive days to two hundred rape victims and encountered no pregnancies, although followup was "difficult."

Progestin Interceptives

Much of the investigational work on the use of progestins alone for postovulatory interception has been done in South America. The most frequently employed agents are dl-Norgestrel and Quingestanol. These drugs have been studied not as a single treatment/emergency therapy interceptive but primarily as an ongoing or recurrent postovulatory interceptive taken immediately after each intercourse.

The contraceptive mechanism of progestins is incompletely understood. The primary action is probably alteration of tubal transport (mainly acceleration).[90, 92, 119] Whether this result is because of a direct progesterone effect on the tube or mediated through an indirect suppressive effect of ovarian progesterone synthesis remains unclear. Theoretically, progestins may also disturb sperm transport and capacitation, thus inhibiting fertilization.[119]

Rubio, et al., employed quingestanol acetate, a progestagen, as a postovulatory interceptive for fertile, married women in a single dose less than twenty-four hours after coitus.[119] Dosages under 0.5mg had little or no interceptive effect. A total of 221 women used a dose of 0.5mg for 927 cycles. Five pregnancies resulted (four drug failures). Two hundred women took 0.8mg for 1,004 cycles and no pregnancies occurred. With the 0.8mg dose the mean number of doses consumed per cycle was 10.6 for an average total drug consumption of 8.5mg per cycle, which is nearly equivalent to the total dose 9.0mg per cycle when the same progestagen is given at 300mcg daily as a "minipill."

A subsequent study by Mischler, et al., used similar doses (0.5mg and 0.75mg) but yielded significantly more pregnancies.[118] The authors attributed the relatively poorer results to the fact that in this study coital frequently was less, therefore the total amount (per menstrual cycle) of progestin ingested was less. When they increased the individual dose of Quingestanol to 1.5 or 2.0mg, the pregnancy rates fell but the incidence of intermenstrual bleeding increased from 10 percent (at the 0.8mg dose) to 35 percent with the 2.0mg dose. This degree of bleeding was felt to be unacceptable by virtue of its adverse affect on compliance. Moggia, et al., gave Quingestanol (1.5mg/dose) or dl-Norgestrel (3.35mg/dose) as recurrent postovulatory interceptives to 879 women with total cycle doses equivalent to those of daily minipills.[120] The pregnancy rates (0.8 to 1.7 percent) were comparable to those observed with daily minipills but the incidence of intermenstrual bleeding was higher. There is no current justification for recommending a progestin-only regime as a single-dose postovulatory interceptive to the sexual assault victim.

Low Dose Estrogen/Progestin Combination Interceptives

Considerable research energy has recently been directed at evaluating the combination of low dose estrogen and progestin as an interceptive (see table 7–3). Yuzpe and associates used a total dose of 100mcg of ethinylestradiol and 1.0mg of dl-Norgestrel (dlN) in 143 women who were within five days of unprotected coital exposure.[123] Three pregnancies resulted (rate = 2.4 percent); two were considered "questionable" treatment failures. Since 1974 when this work was published, a number of investigators have used these compounds but at double the original dose. The usual regime has been to administer two oral contraceptive tablets, each containing 50mcg of ethinylestradiol and 0.5mg of dl-Norgestrel (Ovral[R]— Wyeth Laboratories, Philadelphia, Penn.), immediately and give

Table 7–3
Postovulatory Interception Using a Low Dose
Combination of Ethinylestradiol (EE) and d1-Norgestrel (d1N)

Author	Dosage Regime	Number of Women	Number of Pregnancies	Pregnancy Rate
Yuzpe, et al[123]	(100mcg EE 1.0mg d1N)* × 1	143	3	2.4%
Yuzpe & Lance[91]	(100mcg EE + 1.0mg d1N)* × 2	608	1	0.16%
Shilling[115]	(100mcg EE + 1.0mg d1N) × 2	115	0	0
Yuzpe, et al[86]	(100mcg EE + 1.0mg d1N) × 2	688	7	1.0%
Tully[85]	(100mcg EE + 1.0mg d1N) × 2	395	11	2.0%

* (100mcg EE + 1.0mg d1N) = Two Ovral® tablets (Wyeth Laboratories, Philadelphia, Penn.)

two additional tablets twelve hours later, for a total dose of 200mcg EE and 2.0mg dlN. Subsequent studies have required the same inclusion criteria as the earlier "estrogen only" evaluations; namely, the patient must be within seventy-two hours of a single unprotected episode of intercourse and be free of any contraindications to oral contraceptives.

Yuzpe and Lance treated 608 women and had only one pregnancy (rate 0.16 percent) in which treatment was initiated seventy hours after unprotected coitus.[91] Shilling reported his experience using the same method in 115 coeds and had no pregnancies.[115] Yuzpe and associates expanded their clinical experience in a two-year study with twenty-four participating clinics that eventually enrolled 692 subjects, using double their original dose and limiting exposure to seventy-two hours.[86] Eleven pregnancies resulted, but four were in women who didn't meet inclusion criteria because they had had other unprotected coital exposures during the same cycle. The resultant pregnancy rate for the seven method failures was 1.0 percent. Tully looked retrospectively at 511 patients who received 200mcg EE + 2mg dlN.[85] Only 395 were seen again and eleven pregnancies resulted (rate = 2 percent). All were felt to be method failures.

Ling and associates studied the possible mechanisms of action of low dose estrogen/progestin combinations as postovulatory interceptives.[125] They gave twelve healthy female volunteers 200mcg of EE and 2.0mg of dlN in two divided doses, with the first dose taken at the predicted time of ovulation, and the second twelve hours later. A hormone profile was generated on each subject and an endometrial biopsy was performed about seven days after treatment. The results indicated a broad range of individual variation in hormonal response along the pituitary/ovarian axis. Histological evaluation of the endometrial samplings showed marked alteration of tissue development with dissociation of glandular and stromal maturation. The authors concluded that the postovulatory interceptive effect of this combination was due to suppression of ovulation and/or disrupted luteal functioning via direct effect on the corpus luteum or indirectly by interference with the normal endometrial responses to ovarian steroids.

Adverse Effects of Hormonal Interceptives

Various side effects have been reported with each of the hormonal postovulatory interceptive therapies (see table 7–4). There is considerable similarity in these adverse reactions among the various methods, but the intensity and duration varies with the specific drug and dosage schedule.

Nausea and/or vomiting are by far the most commonly encountered problems. Fifty-two percent to 73 percent of patients given the standard DES treatment (50mg BID for five days) will experience nausea and/or vomiting.[4, 93, 94, 96] Gastrointestinal upset in the ethinylestradiol-treated patients ranged from 12 percent to 78 percent depending on the dosage.[96] Conjugated estrogens also caused a significant degree of nausea and vomiting with the occurrence rates varying from 17 percent to 73 percent.[87, 116, 117] The risk of nausea and vomiting is considerably lower using the low dose EE/dlN method. Reported rates vary from very low (zero to 2 percent) to moderate (42 percent to 60 percent).[85, 86, 91, 115, 123] All seem to agree, however, that even at the higher rates the amount of patient discomfort with EE/dlN method is milder and of shorter duration than with the estrogen-only treatment regimes.

There is good consensus that all patients choosing hormonal

Table 7–4
Frequency of Side Effects Reported after Hormonal Postovulatory Interception

Author	Drug	Dose	Nauseal Vomiting	Menses Early	Menses Late	Irregular Bleeding	Mastalgia
Glover, et al[4]	DES	50mg Daily × 5d	73%				
Kuchera[93]	DES	50mg Daily × 5d	55%	5.2%	12.1%	3.0%	
Kuchera[94]	DES	50mg Daily × 5d	52%	5.5%	12.0%	1.0%	
Haspels[96]	DES	25–50mg Daily × 5d	73%	11.0%	12.0%	9.0%	18%
Haspels[96]	EE	2–5mg Daily × 5d	78%	11.0%	13.0%	11.0%	23%
Lehfeldt[98]	EE	6–25mg Total in 3–5 days	12%*				
Dixon, et al[87]	EE	5mg Daily × 5d	71%			12.0%	
Dixon, et al[87]	CE	30mg Daily × 5d	73%			7.0%	
Notelvitz & Bard[116]	CE	30mg Daily × 5d	67%	19.0%	13.0%	32.0%	27%
Crist[117]	CE	30mg Daily × 5d	17%				
Tully[85]	EE/d1N	200mcg EE + 2.0mg d1N	42%**	31.0%	11.0%		0.3%
Yuzpe, et al[86]	EE/d1N	200mcg EE + 2.0mg d1N	52%**			0.3%	0.6%
Yuzpe, et al[91]	EE/d1N	200mcg EE + 2.0mg d1N	66%**				
Yuzpe[114]	EE/d1N	200mcg EE + 2.0mg d1N	60%**				
Shilling[115]	EE/d1N	200mcg EE + 2.0mg d1N	2%		16%		
Yuzpe, et al[123]	EE/d1N	100mcg EE + 1.0mg d1N	Zero				

Note: DES = Diethylstilbestrol   EE = Ethinylestradiol   CE = Conjugated estrogen   d1N = d1-Norgestrel

* Most patients received very low doses of EE

** Severity and duration of nausea/vomiting was considerably less with EE/d1N groups than with other estrogen only (DES, EE, CE) groups postovulatory interception should receive verbal and written warnings about potential side effects. There is less uniformity regarding the use of antiemetics. Some protocols routinely administer antiemetics prophylactically; others provide them for PRN usage; and still others give them only if requested by the patients because of persistent nausea or vomiting. The decision should be based on the experience of the individual practitioner and the specific treatment method.

Another commonly encountered side effect from hormonal interception is irregular vaginal bleeding (intermenstrual bleeding and/or alteration of normal cycling). DES-treated women reported the onset of the menses following treatment to be earlier than expected in 5.2 percent to 11 percent of cases and later than anticipated in about 12 percent of the cases.[93, 94, 96] Irregular bleeding or spotting in this group ranged from 3 percent to 9 percent. Haspels found his EE-treated group experienced an early menses about 11 percent of the time and a late menses in 13 percent.[96] Irregular bleeding troubled 11 percent of his EE patients. The conjugated estrogen treated group had relatively higher frequencies of bleeding abnormalities with 19 percent reporting an early menses, 13 percent a late menses, and 32 percent some irregular bleeding.[116]

Interceptive therapy with the low dose estrogen/progestin regime produced a broad spectrum of bleeding patterns. The interval between EE/dlN treatment and subsequent menses varied but seemed to be related to time between initiation of treatment and midcycle. If EE/dlN was given at or before midcycle, the next menses tended to be earlier than expected. If treatment was after midcycle, the following menses was often delayed.[123] Apparently none of the vaginal bleeding problems from any method was considered serious or required medical intervention. It behooves the prescribing clinician to discuss the incidence of bleeding abnormalities so the patient can be forewarned that should this side effect occur, it is not likely to require more than patience and reassurance.

Mastalgia may be a bothersome side effect of hormonal therapy. Incidences range from 0.8 percent to 18 percent with DES[93, 94, 96] to 23 percent for ethinylestradiol[96] to as high as 27 percent in women who took conjugated estrogens.[116] A multitude of other

symptoms has been reported by women taking intercep-
tives.[85, 86, 88, 93, 94, 99, 114, 116, 117, 120] The list includes dizziness,
tiredness, malaise, irritability, fatigue, sleep disturbance, faintness,
depression, weight gain, bloating, headache, flatulence, anorexia,
abdominal cramping, and leg cramping. These problems are infrequently or rarely reported. In view of the vague, nonspecific nature
of these complaints caution must be used in assigning a
cause-and-effect relationship with postovulatory interceptive therapy.

The only reported serious side effect was the development of
pulmonary edema in a Miami University coed after three doses of
DES (50mg per day). She cleared within thirty-six hours with
oxygen and supportive therapy.

Method Failures

Regardless of the method chosen or how carefully patients are
screened and selected for postovulatory interceptive therapy,
method failures do occur. Pregnancy is the obvious consequence but
there may be other ramifications. Most clinicians agree that patients
should be warned about the possibility of unsuccessful interception
and be made aware in advance of available resources for pregnancy
termination. It is essential that interceptive patients be instructed
that if menstrual bleeding does not occur within 3 weeks after
completing therapy, they *must* return for pregnancy evaluation.

Ectopic Pregnancy

A disturbing issue raised by some investigators is the apparent
increased incidence of ectopic pregnancy in women who become
pregnant despite interceptive therapy.[85, 88, 90, 92, 96, 97, 99] One investigator, Coutinho, administered depot estradiol (5 to 10mg IM)
to twelve postcoital patients and had two pregnancies develop, both
of which were ectopic.[92] Morris and Van Wagenen reviewed data
from a number of studies and found that nearly 10 percent of
interceptive failure pregnancies were ectopic.[99] This contrasts dra-

matically with the incidence of ectopic in the general population of about 0.5 percent.[92, 99] The mechanism remains uncertain but may be due to altered tubal transport (tubal locking), [90, 92, 97] inhibition of carbonic anthydrase activity,[97, 99] or interference with normal corpus luteum function.[87] Because the total number of reported method failure extrauterine pregnancies is so small (fewer than ten), definitive statistical analysis is not possible. Despite speculation about actual risk and possible mechanisms, it behooves the clinician to discuss this issue with the patient and include it in the informed consent. This potentially lethal problem is one more reason to stress upon the victim the importance of postinterceptive followup.

Subsequent Risk of Cancer or Birth Defects

Another area of concern related to the potential consequences of postovulatory interceptive method failure revolves around the issue of prenatal maternal ingestion of estrogens and subsequent development of clear cell adenocarcinoma of the genital tract in female offspring. In the early 1970s reports began to emerge that implicated DES (previously used to help sustain pregnancy in women with threatened abortion) as a causal factor in genital tract abnormalities of daughters exposed to the drug *in utero*.[121, 122] These findings, coupled with growing public awareness of the problem, probably contributed to an altered perception of the risk, which limited the appeal and use of DES as an interceptive. Two points need to be emphasized. First, women who choose postovulatory interception don't want the pregnancy and most, if not all, who experience method failure opt for abortion.[117] Second, from an embryological standpoint, the risk of carcinogenesis from estrogen exposure only occurs during the oganogenesis of the lower Mullerian tract, which takes place from the fifth to about the seventeenth week.[114, 115] Thus, even in the face of an interceptive failure, the likelihood of a future neoplastic problem occurring is extremely remote.

A related method failure issue is the theoretical risk of teratogenesis in the fetus that implants despite interception. Several reports have suggested an association between intrauterine exposure to female sex hormones and congenital anomalies (primarily con-

genital heart problems and limb reduction defects).[180-183] The
exposures included oral contraceptives, hormone withdrawal tests
for pregnancy, and attempted hormonal therapy for threatened
abortion. Even though some of these exposures were relatively
brief, none was confined to the first seventy-two hours after
conception; all reported abnormalities occurred in fetuses whose
hormone contact took place after nidation. Certainly a potential
risk of teratogenesis following interceptive failure must be acknowledged and shared with the patient, but current data does not
support a direct link.

From a practical standpoint it is appropriate to ask the victim
contemplating interception what she would do in the event of a
method failure pregnancy. If she is certain she would continue the
pregnancy (or even equivocates) it would seem medicolegally
prudent to withhold hormonal therapy.

Hormonal Interceptives and FDA Labeling

Ethinylestradiol, conjugated estrogens, and Ovral[R] are all FDA
approved drugs but their use as interceptives has not been officially
sanctioned. The FDA does still allow the 25mg form of DES to be
used as a postcoital interceptive. However, these 25mg tablets must
be "specifically packaged and accompanied by a patient leaflet fully
explaining the use of the product." (Federal Register, vol. 40, p.
8242, 1975.) Because these 25mg tablets are not currently manu-
factured, the other dosage strengths of DES that are available must
be technically considered as lacking official FDA sanction for
postcoital interception.

The Food, Drug, and Cosmetic Act limits how a drug may be
labeled, promoted, and advertised; it does not limit the manner in
which a physician may use an approved drug. According to the
FDA Drug Bulletin (vol. 121, no. 1, April 1982),

> Once a product has been approved for marketing, a physician
> may prescribe it for uses or treatment regimes or patient popula-
> tions that are not included in approved labeling. Such "unap-
> proved" or, more precisely, "unlabeled" uses may be appropriate

and rational in certain circumstances, and may, in fact, reflect approaches to drug therapy that have been extensively reported in medical literature. . . . accepted medical practice often includes drug use that is not reflected in approved drug labeling.

Hormonal interception with the drugs discussed above would seem to fall within these guidelines. Functionally, it is wise to ensure (via informed consent) that the patient understands interceptives are not technically FDA approved but that their use has been well studied and, to date, found to be safe.

Investigational Drugs

Several agents have recently received consideration as potential postovulatory interceptives. One such drug is danazol, a semisynthetic androgen derivative of ethisterone, which is currently used in the treatment of endometriosis and fibrocystic breast disease. Danazol acts centrally by suppressing the output of gonadotropins (FSH and LH) from the pituitary gland, as well as peripherally by binding to gonadal steroid receptor sites as target organs. Its interceptive effect is incompletely understood but one preliminary trial in England yielded only three pregnancies in 101 women who took the drug after unprotected intercourse.[190] Further research on danazol is needed to more fully evaluate its efficacy and safety.

Another agent under active investigation is the antiprogestational compound miferpristone (RU-486). Unlike danazol, miferpristone exerts no direct effect on the pituitary gland.[184] The antireproductive effect seems to be mediated through competitive binding of progesterone and cortisol receptors.[186] This action is most significant locally in the endometrium.[184] Results from several small clinical trials have been encouraging.[186, 187, 188] Miferpristone seems to be most effective in gestations under eight weeks and it is generally well tolerated, although two patients in one study required curettage and blood transfusion secondary to heavy bleeding.[187] Additional clinical trials are currently under way.

Postcoital IUD Insertion

Insertion of a copper-containing intrauterine device has been shown to be effective postcoital interceptive therapy.[88, 89, 114] As previously discussed, the ovum remains in the fallopian tube for about three days after fertilization. The blastocyst is probably present in the uterus for at least two additional days before implantation is complete.[114] Thus, insertion of an IUD before nidation could prevent implantation and pregnancy. Lippes and associates reported their experience with 299 women who presented to the Buffalo Planned Parenthood Center in need of postcoital interception.[89] All patients had had unprotected intercourse within five days of their visit. A copper-containing IUD was inserted after informed consent was obtained. From 1972 to 1975 a Copper-T was used and from 1975 to 1978 a Copper-7 was inserted. No pregnancies resulted.

This form of mechanical postcoital interception offers several advantages over hormonal therapy. The IUD appears to be effective up to seven days after exposure as compared to only three days with hormonal modalities. The incidence of nausea and vomiting is extremely small after IUD insertion.[89] If the patient so desires, the IUD may be left in place, providing not only emergency interception but also ongoing contraception. Unfortunately, this method is not without potential problems.

Before IUD insertion, pertinent history, exam, and laboratory data should establish the absence of absolute contraindications to IUD use, which include preexisting pregnancy or active upper genital tract infection. In addition, a number of relative contraindications must be considered. History of pelvic inflammatory disease, unresolved abnormal Pap smear, uterine fibroids, history of significant dysmenorrhea, and/or heavy menstrual bleeding may preclude IUD use.

Even if the IUD is to be used for only one cycle strictly as an emergency measure to prevent unwanted pregnancy resulting from a single act of unprotected coitus, the wearer must accept all the risks of insertion and usage. Informed consent for the procedure is mandatory. The risks directly related to insertion are perforation, hemorrhage, and vasovagal reactions. The potential adverse sequela of ongoing IUD use are primarily an increased incidence of pelvic inflammatory disease, infertility (secondary to tubal scarring from salpingitis), and an increased probability of ectopic pregnancy.[133, 134, 135, 136]

Considerable controversy exists in the medical literature regarding the magnitude of these ongoing risks and the interrelationships of a number of operant variables (age, parity, number of sexual partners, duration of IUD usage, etc). An additional caveat in the context of postassault interception is the potential for enhanced risk of venereal disease transmission. Cervicouterine instrumentation in this setting could theoretically increase the likelihood of developing pelvic inflammatory disease. Some authorities, therefore, do not recommend postcoital IUD usage in the rape victim.[135] There is consensus, however, that the patient must be aware of these problems and willing to accept the risks if an intrauterine device is to be inserted.

In January 1986, G. D. Searle & Company announced that they would discontinue the production of both Copper-7s and Copper-Ts. Because IUD interception has only been studied with these two copper-containing devices, this method has effectively been eliminated. Two potential alternatives may still exist, however. First, some institutions may have a leftover supply of Copper-7s and/or Copper-Ts, which could be used until their expiration dates are reached. Second, the only IUD still marketed in the United States is the Progestasert-T[R] (ALZA Corporation). Although to date it has not been investigated as an interceptive, future studies may show it to be effective and, thus, restore IUD interception to the list of postcoital contraceptive alternatives.

Sexually Transmitted Disease

The sexual assault victim is potentially at risk for contracting any sexually transmitted disease (see figure 7–2). According to the Centers for Disease Control, the most likely diseases that rape victims contract are chlamydial infections, gonorrhea, genital herpes, cytomegalovirus (CMV), trichomonas, and possibly syphilis and hepatitis B.[129] There is currently not adequate prophylaxis for herpes simplex or CMV infections. Administration of hepatitis B

Chlamydial Infections
Gonorrhea
Genital Herpes
Cytomegalovirus Infections
Trichomoniasis
Syphilis
Hepatitis B

Figure 7–2. *Most Common Sexually Transmitted Disease Acquired during Sexual Assault*[129]

immune globulin is recommended only in situations where there is a high index of suspicion of exposure. Morbidity from trichomonas is extremely low. Increasing awareness and improved laboratory methodology have brought to light the fact that chlamydia trachomatis infections are the most prevalent sexually transmitted diseases in the United States today.[129] The potential for acquiring syphilis and gonorrhea from rape has long been recognized.

Chlamydia

Chlamydia trachomatis has been shown to produce a host of sexually transmitted genitourinary infections, including prostatitis, cervicitis, urethritis, and pelvic inflammatory disease.[127] Chlamydia is currently the most prevalent sexually transmitted bacterial pathogen in the country.[129] In the last several years laboratory methods for the detection of chlamydia have become less expensive and more widely available. Despite this trend, diagnosis and treatment of these infections is still frequently based on clinical grounds.

Another important factor to consider is the high frequency of coexisting chlamydial and gonorrhea infections. Available data suggest that 25 percent to 50 percent of patients with positive gonorrhea cultures will also have positive laboratory evidence of chlamydia.[127, 129] In the context of the sexual assault victim, two recommendations have been advanced. First, when available, a chlamydia test should be obtained from any potentially infected site. Second, if STD prophylaxis is initiated, the regime should include adequate treatment for chlamydia. The current first-line drugs for chlamydia are tetracycline (500mg QID × seven days), doxycycline (100mg BID × seven days) or erythromycin (500mg QID × seven days).[129] If single-dose prophylaxis against gonorrhea and syphilis is used, it should be followed by one of the above regimes. Doxycycline is probably the best alternative because it produces the least gastrointestinal upset, is only minimally affected by food in the GI tract and offers the best chance for good compliance by way of its BID dosage schedule.

Gonorrhea

Gonorrhea is an extremely common infection with an estimated three million new cases per years.[127] It is highly contagious, with 50 to 90 percent of single exposures resulting in infection, and has a short incubation period (only two to five days), which allows for rapid turnover of infected "generations."[127] The likelihood of developing a positive gonorrhea culture as the result of sexual assault varies from 3 percent to 9 percent.[7, 8, 9, 14, 15, 19, 130, 132, 137] All rape victims should be made aware of this hazard and be offered the option of prophylaxis at the time of the evidentiary exam.

Some women may choose to defer treatment until their follow-up visit, when the culture results are available. Many clinicians, however, favor encouraging early prophylaxis because of high failure rate for postassault followup.[19] Poor compliance has thus prompted many examiners to strongly recommend that the victim accept a single dose therapy against gonorrhea and incubating syphilis before leaving the emergency department.

Most authorities concur with and follow the treatment guidelines for sexually transmitted diseases set forth by the Centers for Disease Control (see table 7–5).[129] Aqueous procaine penicillin G (APPG) given intramuscularly (4.8 million units) plus 1.0gm of probenecid by mouth has been a standard therapy for years. Amoxicillin (3.0gm) or ampicillin (3.5gm) orally plus 1.0gm of probenecid has also been an effective single dose prophylaxis against gonorrhea. The emergence of penicillinase-producing *Neisseria gonorrhoeae* (PPNG) and concurrent chlamydial infections has influenced many clinicans to additionally recommend tetracycline (500mg QID) or doxycycline (100mg BID) for seven days.

If fellatio was involved in the assault it should be noted that the

Table 7-5
Prophylaxis against Sexually Transmitted Diseases Potentially Acquired by the Sexual Assault Victim

Drug	Route	Dosage	Duration	Neisseria Gonorrhea			Chlamydia trachomatis	Incubating Syphilis
				Urogenital	Pharyngeal	Rectal		
Aqueous Procaine Penicillin G plus: Probenecid.	IM / PO	4.8 × 10⁶ units / 1.0 gm	Once / Once	Effective	Effective	Effective	Not Effective	Effective
Amoxicillin plus: Probenecid	PO / PO	3.0 gm / 1.0 gm	Once / Once	Effective	Not Effective	*	Not Effective	Insufficient Data
Ampicillin plus: Probenecid	PO / PO	3.5 gm / 1.0 gm	Once / Once	Effective	Not Effective	*	Not Effective	Insufficient Data
Ceftriaxone	IM	250 mg	Once	Effective	Effective	Effective	Not Effective	Insufficient Data
Spectinomycin	IM	2.0 gm	Once	Effective	Not Effective	Effective	Not Effective	Not Effective
Cefotaxime	IM	1.0 gm	Once	Effective		Effective	Not Effective	
Cefoxitin plus: Probenecid	IM / PO	2.0 gm / 1.0 gm	Once / Once	Effective	Not Effective	Effective	Not Effective	
Cefuroxime plus: Probenecid	IM / PO	1.5 gm / 1.0 gm	Once / Once	Effective			Not Effective	
Tetracycline HCl**	PO	500 mg QID	7 days / 15 days	Effective	Effective	*	Effective	Effective
Doxycycline Hyclate**	PO	100mg BID	7 days / 15 days	Effective	Effective	*	Effective	Effective
Erythromycin	PO	500 mg QID	7 days / 15 days	Effective			Effective	
Trimethoprim (80mg) + Sulfamethofazole(400mg)	PO	9 Tablets Daily	5 days	Effective			Insufficient Data	

* Probably effective in women; not effective in men
** Not to be used in pregnancy because of adverse effects on fetus

Legend: Effective | Probably Effective | Insufficient Data

single dose therapies using amoxicillin or ampicillin are not effective in eradicating pharyngeal gonorrhea, so the tetracycline/doxycycline or injectable penicillin treatment schedule should be used. The best alternatives for the penicillin allergic patient are tetracycline-/doxycycline or erythromycin. If a tetracycline cannot be used, alternatives include spectinomycin (2gm IM once), ceftriaxone (250mg IM once), cefoxitin (2gm IM once) plus 1.0gm of probenecid orally, or cefotaxine (1.0gm IM once).

Syphilis

Infection with the treponemal organism *T. pallidum* causes syphilis. The incidence of syphilis is much less than gonorrhea with an estimated twenty-five thousand to fifty thousand cases occurring per year.[127] The total number of cases has remained relatively stable during recent years but there has been an alarming shift, with a sharp increase in cases occurring in the male homosexual population. Syphilis is significantly less contagious than gonorrhea. Probably fewer than one third of individuals exposed will develop the disease.[127] The risk of contracting syphilis from a sexual assault has generally been found to be about 0.1 percent[7, 9, 83] A nontreponimal screening test (VDRL or RPR) should be drawn at the time of the evidentiary exam and repeated in six weeks. The test is indicated not for initial management but to help establish the victim's serologic status at the time of the assault.[130] Incubating syphilis (seronegative without clinical signs of disease) is effectively treated by procaine penicillin/probenecid regime used for gonorrhea and is probably cured by amoxicillin, ampicillin or tetracycline as described above.[127, 128, 129] It will not be eradicated by spectinomycin.

Sexual Assault and Acquired Immune Deficiency Syndrome (AIDS)

Acquired Immunodeficiency Syndrome (AIDS) is a sexually transmissible infection caused by a retrovirus currently designated as human immunodeficiency virus (HIV). It has also been called human T-cell lymphotropic virus type III/lymphadenopathy—

associated virus (HTLV-III/LAV). Infection with this virus suppresses T-helper lymphocytes and renders the host susceptible to a variety of immune disturbances, serious opportunistic infections, and malignancies. Factors that influence susceptibility to HIV infection, the development of overt disease, and eventual outcome are incompletely understood and the subject of an intense worldwide research effort. Current literature suggests that about 5 percent of infected individuals will ultimately develop AIDS, while a larger percentage will develop AIDS-related conditions.[129] It is unknown what percentage HIV antibody positive individuals ultimately develop AIDS over a lifetime of infection. To date, no intervention has proved effective in altering the course of HIV infection, curing the patient with overt AIDS, or reversing the immunoincompetence produced by the virus.

Because HIV can unquestionably be transmitted by sexual contact, the risk of contracting AIDS is of obvious concern to the victim of sexual assault. Unfortunately, there is no currently available method to ascertain the degree of risk. At present, there are no specific recommendations for evaluating either the rape victim or the assailant for HIV antibody status. If the convicted assailant was found to belong to a high-risk group (homosexual, bisexual, intravenous drug abuser) it would not be unreasonable to test the antibody status of both victim and assailant and follow both depending on the results.

Evidentiary Examination Followup

Two followup visits are generally recommended after the evidentiary exam.[7, 9, 137] Specific injuries or special problems may require additional contact. The first visit is scheduled for two weeks after the initial exam, at which time a repeat gonorrhea culture is obtained and laboratory data are reviewed. This also offers an excellent opportunity to answer any questions the victim has and assess her general wellbeing and degree of adjustment to the trauma she has endured. If indicated and not already arranged, referral for counseling may be expedited at this time. The second visit should be about six weeks after the attack. Repeat gonorrhea culture, repeat VDRL or RPR, and urine pregnancy tests are performed. Any positive laboratory findings should be dealt with appropriately. Again, the clinician should be sensitive to the psychological needs of the victim and offer support and referral when needed.

8
Conclusion

Rape is much more than a coerced sexual act; it is a violent, brutal, and dehumanizing attack on body and spirit. The consequences may be lasting physical and emotional injuries which affect not only the victim but those around her. Sexual assault is the most rapidly growing violent crime in America, but reported offenses probably account for only a small portion of the total problem. Our history is replete with myth and misconception about rape and its victims. Sex role stereotypes and antiquated laws have effectively prevented the rape victim from receiving adequate remedies for her unique legal, medical, and emotional needs. Those in the law enforcement, judicial, and medical establishments who are responsible for aiding the sexual assault victim have not always responded optimally. Unfortunately, the victim's ordeal may not end with the departure of the rapist but continue as she proceeds through the medical and criminal justice systems.

The last fifteen years have seen rapid changes in many areas related to sexual assault. The feminist movement has been instrumental in educating the public and increasing awareness about the realities of rape and the true plight of its victims. Traditional sex roles are disappearing; stereotypes are weakening; rape reform legislation is well supported and widespread. Better training for those who must interact with the sexually assaulted individual has helped achieve more sensitive and compassionate treatment for victims. Technological advancement in medical and forensic science offer the victim not only a better chance for remaining healthy, but also ever-improving odds for obtaining justice. Enhanced understanding about the psychological needs of the victim has stimulated the development of a variety of counseling services and support groups now available in most communities.

The role of the clinician who cares for the sexual assault victim is unique in clinical medicine. The medical examiner must accept responsibilities not only to the patient but also to the criminal justice system. The provision of comprehensive medical care and appropriate followup are traditional objectives in the medical encounter. The clinician who participates in the evaluation of the rape victim must take on the added duties of forensic investigator and expert witness. The challenges are often substantial but need not be overwhelming. Proper training and experience will provide insight into the complexities of the evidential exam. Understanding and compassion will help ensure the wellbeing of the victim and see that justice is served.

Notes

1. Woodling, B.A.; Evans, J.R.; Bradbury, M.D. "Sexual assault: rape and molestation." *Clin. Obstet. Gynecol.* 20:509–530, 1977.
2. Talbert, S.; White, S.D.; Bowen, J.D.; et al. "Improving emergency department care of the sexual assault victim." *Ann. Emerg. Med.* 9:293–297, 1980.
3. Cryer, L.; Mattox, K.L. "Rape evidence kit: Simplified procedures for the emergency department." *JACEP.* 5:890–893, 1976.
4. Glover, D.; Gerety, M.; Bromberg, S; et al. "Diethylstilbestrol in the treatment of rape victims." *West. J. Med.* 125:331–334, 1976.
5. Fahrney, P.M. "Sexual assault package: Refinement of a previous idea." *JACEP.* 4:340–341, 1975.
6. Pepitone–Rockwell, F. "Patterns of rape and approaches to care." *J. Fam. Prac.* 6:521–529, 1978.
7. Sweeney, P.J. "Enlightened management of the rape victim" (two parts). *ER Reports.* 2:91–98, Sept./Oct., 1981.
8. Evrard, J.R.; Gold, E.M. "Epidemiology and management of sexual assault victims." *Obstet. Gynecol.* 53:381–387, 1979.
9. Braen, G.R. "The rape examination." North Chicago, Ill., Abbott Laboratories, 1976.
10. Shiff, A.F. "How to handle the rape victim." *South. Med. J.* 71:509–511, 1978.
11. Pollack, M.S.; Shafer, I.A.; Barford, D.; Dupont, B, et al. "Prenatal identification of paternity: HLA typing helpful after rape." *JAMA.* 244–246, 1954, 1980.
12. Hicks, D.L. "Rape: sexual assault." *Am. J. Obstet. Gynecol.* 137:931–935, 1980.
13. Bassuk, E.; Savitz, R.; McCombie, S.; et al. "Organizing a rape crisis program in a general hospital." *JAMWA.* 30:486–490, 1975.
14. Soules, M.R.; Stewart, S.K.; Brown, K.M.; et al. "The spectrum of alleged rape." *J. Reprod. Med.* 20:33–39, 1978.
15. Tedeschi, D.G.; Eckert, W.G.; Tedeshi, L.G. In *Forensic Medicine*, volume 2, chapter 37: "Rape." Published by W. B. Saunders, 1977.
16. Paul, D.M. "The medical examination of the live rape victim and the accused." *Legal Med. Ann.* 137–153, 1977.

17. California Medical Association Committee on Evolving Trends in Society Affecting Life and the Advisory Panels of Obstetrics and Gynecology, Pathology, and Psychiatry of the Scientific Board of the California Medical Association. "Guidelines for the Interview and Examination of Alleged Rape Victims." *West. J. Med.* 123:420–422, 1975.

18. Sternbaugh, G.L. "Treatment of rape victims." *Emerg. Med. Services.* Jan/Feb., 8–15, 1976.

19. Halbert, D.R.; Darnell-Jones, D.E. "Medical management of the sexually assaulted woman." *J. Reprod. Med.* 20:265–274, 1978.

20. State of California, Department of Justice, Bureau of Forensic Services. Guidelines for Physical Evidence in Sexual Assault Investigations. July 1980.

21. Davies, A.; Wilson, E. "The persistence of seminal constituents in the human vagina." *J. Forensic Sci.* 3:45–55, 1974.

22. Findley, T.P. "Quantitation of vaginal acid phosphatase and its relationship to time of coitus." *Am. J. Clin. Pathol.* 68:238–242, 1977.

23. Soules, M.R.; Pollard, A.A.; Brown, K.M.; Mool, V. "The forensic laboratory evaluation of evidence in alleged rape." *"Am. J. Obstet. Gynecol.* 130;142–146, 1978.

24. Silverman, E.M.; Silverman, A.G. "The persistence of spermatozoa in the lower genital tracts of women." *JAMA.* 240;1875–1877, 1978.

25. Gomez, R.F.; Wunsch, C.D.; Davis, J.H.; Hicks, D.J. "Qualitative and quantitative determinations of acid phosphatase activity in vaginal washings." *Am. J. Clin. Pathol.* 64:423–432, 1975.

26. Sensabaugh, G.F. "The quantitative acid phosphatase test. A statistical analysis of endogenous and postcoital acid phosphatase levels in the vagina." *J. Forensic Sci.* 24:346–365, 1979.

27. Enos, W.F.; Beyer, J.C. "Prostatic acid phosphatase, aspermia, and alcoholism in rape cases." *J. Forensic Sci.* 25:353–356, 1980.

28. Duenhoelter, J.H.; Stone, I.C.; Santos-Ramos, R.; Scott, D.E. "Detection of seminal fluid constituents after alleged sexual assault." *J. Forensic Sci.* 23:824–829, 1978.

29. Schumann, B.G.; Badawy, S.; Peglow, A.; Henry, J.B.; et al. "Prostatic acid phosphatase. Current assessment in vaginal fluid of alleged rape victims." *Am. J. Clin. Pathol.* 66:944–952, 1976.

30. Enos, W.F.; Beyer, J.D. "Spermatozoa in the anal canal and rectum and in the oral cavity of female rape victims." *J. Forensic Sci.* 23:231–233, 1978.

31. Davies, A. Discussion of "Spermatozoa in the anal canal and rectum and in the oral cavity of female rape victims." *J. Forensic Sci.* 24:541–542, 1979 (Letter).

32. Burgess, A.; Holmstrom, L. "Rape Trauma Syndrome." *Am. J. Psychiatry.* 131:981–986, 1974.

33. Pole, K. "The medical examination in sexual offenses." *Med. Sci. Law.* 16:73–74, 1976.

34. Shiff, A. "A statistical evaluation of rape." *J. Forensic Sci.* 2:339–349, 1973.

35. Paul, D.M. "The medical examination in sexual offenses." *Med. Sci. Law.* 15:154–162, 1975.
36. Groth, A.N.; Burgess, A.W. "Sexual dysfunction during rape." *NEJM.* 297:764–766, 1977.
37. Rabkin, J.G. "Epidemiology of forcible rape." *Am. J. Orthopsychiatry.* 49:634–647, 1979.
38. Groth, A.N.; Burgess, A.W.; Holmstrom, L.L. "Rape: Power, Anger and Sexuality." *Am. J. Psychiatry.* 134:1239–1243, 1977.
39. Burgess, A.W.; Holmstrom, L.L. "Rape: Sexual disruption and recovery." *Am. J. Orthopsychiatry.* 49:648–657, 1979.
40. Kilpatric, D.G.; Veronen, L.J.; Resick, P.A.; et al. "The aftermath of rape: Recent empirical findings. *Am. J. Orthopsychiatry.* 49:658–669, 1979.
41. Shiff, A.F. "Rape in the United States." *J. Forensic Sci.* 23:845–851, 1978.
42. Root, I.; Ogden, W.; Scott, W. "The medical investigation of alleged rape." *West. J. Med.* 120:329–333, 1974.
43. McCloskey, K.L.; Muscillo, G.C.; Noordewier, B.; et al. "Prostatic acid phosphatase activity in the postcoital vagina." *J. Forensic Sci.* 20:630–636, 1975.
44. Morrison, A.I. "Persistence of spermatozoa in the vagina and cervix." *Br. J. Venereal Dis.* 48:141–143, 1972.
45. Blake, E.T.; Sensabaugh, G.F. "Genetic markers in semen: A review." *J. Forensic Sci.* 21:784–796, 1976.
46. Blake, E.T.; Sensabaugh, F. "Genetic markers in human semen: II: Quantitation of polymorphic proteins." *J. Forensic Sci.* 23:717–729, 1978.
47. Enos, W.F.; Beyer, J.C. "Treatment of rape victims." *J. Forensic Sci.* 22:3–4, 1977.
48. Hamburg, D.; Adams, J.E. "A perspective of coping behavior." *Arch. Gen. Psych.* 17:277–284, 1967.
49. Martin, C.A.; Warfield, M.C.; Braen, G.R. "Physician's management of the psychological aspects of rape." *JAMA.* 249:501–503, 1983.
50. Notman, M.T.; Nadelson, C.C. "The rape victim: Psychodynamic considerations." *Am. J. Psychiatry.* 133:408–413, 1976.
51. Burgess, A.W.; Holmstrom, L.L. "Coping behavior of the rape victim." *Am. J. Psychiatry.* 133:413–418, 1976.
52. Sutherland, S.; Scherl, D. "Patterns of response among victims of rape." *Am. J. Orthopsychiatry.* 40:503–511, 1970.
53. Hicks, D.J. "Rape: Sexual assault." *Obstet. Gynecol. Annual.* 7:447–465, 1978.
54. Andreasen, N.C. "Post-traumatic Stress Disorder." In Kaplan, H.I.; Freedman, A.M.; Sadock, B.J. (eds.): *Comprehensive Textbook of Psychiatry,* III. Published by Williams & Wilkins Co., Baltimore, volume 2, 1517–1525, 1980.
55. Rape and related offenses. Crime Charging Standards, Section 324 California District Attorney's Association, 1982.
56. U.S. Government Printing Office: Uniform Crime Reports, 1960, 1970, 1980.

57. Bohmer, C.; Blumberg, A. "Twice traumatized: The rape victim and the court." *Judicature.* 58:391–399, 1975.
58. Lindemann, E. "Symptomatology and management of acute grief." *Am. J. Psychiatry.* 101:141–148, 1944.
59. Brownmiller, S. *Against Our Will: Men, Women and Rape.* New York, Simon, 1975.
60. Burgess, A.W.; Holmstrom, L.L. "The rape victim in the emergency ward." *Am. J. Nursing.* 73:1740–1745, 1973.
61. ———. "Crisis and counseling requests of rape victims." *Nursing Res.* 23:196–202, 1974.
62. Masters, W.H.; Johnson, V.E. *Textbook of Sexual Medicine.* Boston, Little Brown & Co. 427–446, 1979.
63. Symonds, M. "Victims of violence: Psychological effects and aftereffects." *Am. J. Psychoanalysis.* 35:19–26, 1975.
64. Paul, D.M. "Medical examination of the live rape victim and the accused." *Med. Trial. Tech.* Q:424–442, Spring 1982.
65. Pollak, O.J. "Semen and seminal stains." *Arch. Pathol.* 35:140–187, 1943.
66. Sharpe, N. "The significance of spermatozoa in victims of sexual offenses." *Can. Med. Assoc. J.* 89:513–514, 1963.
67. Rupp, J.C. "Sperm survival and prostatic acid phosphatase activity in victims of sexual assault." *J. Forensic Sci.* 14:177–183, 1969.
68. Smally, A.J. "Sperm and acid phosphatase examination of the rape patient: Medicolegal aspects." *J. Fam. Pract.* 15:170–171, 1982.
69. Wallace-Haagens, M.J.; Duffy, B.J.; Holtrop, H.R. "Recovery of spermatozoa from human vaginal washings." *Fertil. Steril.* 26:175–179, 1975.
70. Wecht, C.H.; Collom, W.D. "Medical evidence in alleged rape." *Legal Med. Ann.* 269–285, 1969.
71. Massey, J.B.; Garcia, C.R.; Emich, J.P. "Management of sexually assaulted females." *Obstet. Gynecol.* 38:29–35, 1971.
72. Austin, C.R. "Sperm fertility, viability and persistence in the female tract." *J. Reprod. Fertil.* (suppl) 22:75–89, 1975.
73. Perloff, W.H. "Steinberger: In vivo survival of spermatozoa in cervical mucous." *Am. J. Obstet. Gynecol.* 88:439–442, 1964.
74. Lantz, R.K.; Eisenberg, R.B. "Preservation of acid phosphatase activity in medicolegal specimens." *Clin. Chem.* 24;486–488, 1978.
75. Masood, S.; Bernhardt, H.E.; Sager, N.; et al. "Quantitative determination of endogenous acid phosphatase activity in vaginal washings." *Obstet. Gynecol.* 51:33–36, 1978.
76. Dahlke, M.B.; Cooke, C.; Cunnane, M.; et al. "Identification of semen in 500 patients seen because of rape." *Am. J. Clin. Pathol.* 68;740–746, 1977.
77. Schelble, D.T.; Bradford, J.C. "An 18-month evaluation of the Akron General Medical Center Assault/Rape Protocol." *Ann. Emerg. Med.* 11:9–17, 1982.
78. Price, C.J.; Davies, A.; Wraxall, B.G.D.; et al. "The typing of phosphogluco-mutase in vaginal material and semen." *J. Forensic Sci.* 16:29–42, 1976.

79. Issitt, P.D.; Issitt, C.H.; *Applied Blood Group Serology.* Oxnard, Calif., Becton, Dickinson, and Co., 1976 (241–242, 31–32, 78–79).
80. Wertheimer, A.J. "Examination of the rape victim." *Post Grad. Med.* 71:173–180, 1982.
81. Jensen vs. State, 153, N.W. 2d 566 (Wisc. 1967).
82. Smith, S.; Cook, W.G.H. (ed.) *Taylor's Principles and Practice of Medical Jurisprudence.* Eighth ed., volume 2, 133–136, Churchill, London, 1928.
83. Frenkel, D.A. "Sperm migration and survival in the endometrial cavity." *Int. J. Fert.* 6:285–290, 1961.
84. Tagatz, G.E.; Okagaki, T.; Sciarra, J.S. "The effect of vaginal lubricants on sperm motility and viability in vitro." *Am. J. Obstet. Gynecol.* 113:88–90, 1972.
85. Tully, B. "Postcoital contraception—a study." *Br. J. Fam. Plan.* 8:119–124, 1983.
86. Yuzpe, A.A.; Smith, R.P.; Rademaker, W.W. "A multicenter clinical investigation employing ethinylestradiol combined with dl-Norgestrel as a postcoital contraceptive agent." *Fertil. Steril.* 37:508–513, 1982.
87. Dixon, G.W.; Schlesselman, J.J.; Ory, H.W.; et al. "Ethinylestradiol and conjugated estrogens as postcoital contraceptives." *JAMA.* 244:1336–1339, 1980.
88. (Anonymous). "Postcoital Contraception." *Lancet.* 476–83, April 16, 1983.
89. Lippes, J.; Tatum, H.J.; Maulik, D.; et al. "Postcoital copper IUDs." Association of Planned-Parenthood Physicians. XIV:3:87–94, 1979.
90. Aref, I.; Hafez, S.E. "Postcoital contraception: Physiological and clinical parameters." *Obstet. Gynecol. Survey.* 32;417–437, 1977.
91. Yuzpe, A.A.; Lance, W.J. "Ethinylestradiol and dl-Norgestrestel as a postcoital contraceptive." *Fertil. Steril.* 9:932–936, 1977.
92. Blye, R.P. "The use of estrogens as postcoital contraceptive agents." *Am. J. Obstet. Gynecol.* 116:1044–1050, 1973.
93. Kuchera, L.K. "Postcoital contraception with diethylstilbestrol." *JAMA.* 218:562–563, 1971.
94. ———. "Postcoital contraception with diethylstilbestrol—Updated." *Contraception.* 10:47–54, 1974.
95. Tietze, C. "Probability of pregnancy resulting from a single unprotected coitus." *Fertil. Steril.* 11:485–488, 1960.
96. Haspels, A.A. "Interception: Postcoital estrogens in 3,016 women." *Contraception.* 14:375–381, 1976.
97. Smythe, A.R.; Underwood, P.B. "Ectopic pregnancy after postcoital diethylstilbestrol." *Am. J. Obstet. Gynecol.* 121:284–285, 1975.
98. Lehfeldt, H. "Choice of ethinylestradiol as a postcoital pill." *Am. J. Obstet. Gynecol.* 116:892–893, 1973.
99. Morris, J.M.; Van Wagenen, G. "Interception: The use of postovulatory estrogens to prevent implantation." *Am. J. Obstet. Gynecol.* 115:101–106, 1973.

100. Schwartz, D.; Mayaux, M.J.; Martin-Boyce, A.; et al. "Donor insemination: Conception rate according to cycle day in a series of 821 cycles with a single insemination." *Fertil. Steril.* 31:226–229, 1979.

101. Riisfeldt, O. "Acid phosphatase employed as a new method of demonstrating seminal spots in forensic medicine." *Acta. Pathol. Microbiol. Scand. Sppl.* 58:1–80, 1946.

102. Sumner, N.A.; Brush, M.G. "Isoenzymes of acid phosphate in the human endometrium." *Biochem. J.* 128:103–104, 1972.

103. Willott, G.M. "L-tartrate inhibitable acid phosphatase in semen and vaginal secretions." *J. Forensic Sci. Soc.* 12:363–366, 1972.

104. Allard, J.; Davies, A. "Further information on the use of p-nitrophenyl phosphate to quantitate acid phosphatase on vaginal swabs examined in cases of sexual assault." *Med. Sci. Law.* 19:170–173, 1979.

105. Nun, S.; Musacchio, L.; Epstein, J.A. "Variations in seminal plasma constituents from fertile, subfertile and vasectomized azoospermic men." *Fert. Steril.* 23:357–360, 1972.

106. Sesabaugh, G.F. "Isolation and characterization of a semen-specific protein from human seminal plasma: a potential new marker for semen identification." *J. Forensic Sci.* 23:106–115, 1978.

107. Pinto, F.C. "Rape: For the defense . . . Acid phosphatase." *J. Forensic Med.* 6:147–159, 1959.

108. Barrett, J.C.; Marshall, J. "Risk of conception on different days of the menstrual cycle." *Popul. Stud.* 3:455–461, 1967.

109. Vollman, R.F. "Assessment of the fertile and sterile phases of the menstrual cycle." *Int. Review of Nat. Fam. Plan.* 1:40–47, 1977.

110. Bark, J.E.; Harris, J.M.; Firth, M. "Typing of the common phosphogluco-motase variants using isoelectric focusing—A new interpretation of the phosphoglucomotase system. *J. Forensic Sci. Soc.* 16:115–120, 1976.

111. Sensabaugh, G.F.; Golden, V.L.; Esterase, D. "Polymorphism in Chinese and Japanese." *Human Genetics.* 36:267–271, 1973.

112. Caldwell, K.; Blake, E.T.; Sensabaugh, G.F. "Sperm diaphorase: Genetic polymorphism of a sperm-specific enzyme in man." *Science* (Washington, D.C.). 191:1185–1187, 1976.

113. Burton, M.J. "Hairs and fibers as evidence." *Med. Leg. Bull.* 25:1, 1976.

114. Yuzpe, A.A. "Postcoital contraception." *Int. J. Gynecol. Obstet.* 16:497–501, 1979.

115. Shilling, L.H. "An alternative to the use of high dose estrogen for postcoital contraception." *JACHA.* 27:247–249, 1979.

116. Notelovitz, M.; Bard, D. "Conjugated estrogen as a postovulatory intercep-tive." *Contraception.* 17:443–454, 1978.

117. Crist, T.; Farrington, C. "The use of estrogen as a postcoital contraceptive in North Carolina—Trick or Treatment." *NC Med. J.* 34:792–795, 1973.

118. Mischler, T.W.; Rubio, B.; Larrañaga, A.; et al. "Further experience with

quingestanol acetate as a postcoital oral contraceptive." *Contraception.* 9:221–225, 1974.

119. Rubio, B.; Berman, E.; Larrañaga, A.; et al. "A new postcoital oral contraceptive." *Contraception.* 1:303–314, 1970.

120. Moggia, A.; Beauqis, A.; Ferrari, F.; et al. "The use of progestogens as postcoital oral contraceptives." *J. Reprod. Med.* 13:58–61, 1974.

121. Herbst, A.L.; Robboy, S.J.; Scully, R.E.; et al. "Clear-cell adenocarcinoma of the vagina and cervix of girls: analysis of 170 registry cases." *Am. J. Obstet. Gynec.* 119:713–724, 1974.

122. Herbst, A.L.; Poskanzer, D.C.; Robboy, S.J.; et al. "Prenatal exposure to stilbestrol." *NEJM.* 292:334–339, 1975.

123. Yuzpe, A.A.; Thurlow, H.J.; Ramzy, I.; et al. "Postcoital contraception—a pilot study." *J. Repro. Med.* 13:53–59, 1974.

124. Lippes, J.; Malik, T.; Tatum, H.J. "The postcoital copper." *T. Adv. Planned Parent.* 11:24–29, 1976.

125. Ling, W.Y.; Robichaud, A.; Zayid, I.; et al. "Mode of action of dl-Norgestrel and ethinylestradiol combination in postcoital contraception." *Fertil. Steril.* 32:297–302, 1979.

126. Grenwald, P.; Barlow, J.J.; Nasca, P.C.; et al. "Vaginal cancer after maternal treatment with synthetic estrogens." *NEJM.* 285:390–392, 1971.

127. Lynch, P.J. "Therapy of sexually transmitted diseases." *Med. Clinics of North Am.* 66:915–925, 1982.

128. Abramowicz, M. (editor). "Treatment of sexually transmitted diseases." *Medical Letter.* 24:29–34, 1982.

129. "Sexually transmitted diseases: Treatment guidelines." Centers for Disease Control, *Morbid Mortal Wkly. Rep.* (supplement). volume 31, 20 August 1982.

130. Hayman, C.R. "Serologic tests for syphilis in rape cases." *JAMA.* 228:1227–1228, 1974.

131. Hayman, C.R.; Lanza C. "Sexual assault on women and girls." *Am. J. Obstet. Gynecol.* 109:480–486, 1971.

132. Hayman, C.R.; Lanza, C.; Fuentes, R.; et al. "Rape in the District of Columbia." *Am. J. Obstet. Gynecol.* 113:91–97, 1972.

133. Burkman, R.T. "Intrauterine device use and the risk of pelvic inflammatory disease." *Am. J. Obstet. Gynecol.* 138:861–863, 1980.

134. Ory, H.W. "Ectopic pregnancy and intrauterine contraceptive devices: New perspectives." *Obstet. Gynecol.* 57:137–144, 1981.

135. Burkman, R.T. "Association between intrauterine device and pelvic inflammatory disease." *Obstet. Gynecol.* 57:269–276, 1981.

136. Malhorta, N.; Chaudhury, R.R. "Current status of intrauterine devices: Pelvic inflammatory disease and ectopic pregnancy." *Obstet. Gynecol. Survey.* 37:1–7, 1982.

137. Breen, J.L.; Greenwald, E. "Rape." In Glass, R.H., *Office Gynecology.* 184–200. Baltimore: Williams & Wilkins, 1976.

138. Hatcher, R.A.; Stewart, G.K.; Stewart, F.G.; et al. *Contraceptive Technology: 1982–1983.* 72–96, 155–196. Irvington Publishers, Inc, New York. 1983.

139. Bienen, L. "Rape III: National developments in rape reform legislation." 6 *Women's Rights L. Rep.* 170–213, Spring 1980.

140. Schwartz, M.D. "The spousal exemption for criminal rape prosecution." *Vermont Law Review,* 33–57, Spring 1982.

141. Barrows, T.R. "Abolishing the marital exemption for rape: A statutory proposal." *Univ. Ill. Law Review.* 201–228, Winter 1983.

142. Graham, M.H. "Relevancy and the exclusion of relevant evidence— The federal rape shield statute." 18 *Crim. Law Bull.* 513–523, Nov.–Dec., 1982.

143. Mirabile, P.J. "Rape laws, equal protection and privacy rights." 54 *Tulane L. Rev.* 456–479, February 1980.

144. Friedman, D.J. "Rape corroboration requirement: Repeal not reform." 81 *Yale Law J.* 1365–1391, 1972.

145. McShane, P.M.; Schiff, I.; Trentham, D.E. "Cellular immunity to sperm in infertile women." *JAMA.* 253:3555–3558, 1985.

146. Sensabaugh, G.F.; Bashinski, J.; Blake, E.T. "The laboratory's role in investigating rape." *Diagnostic Medicine.* 46–53, March 1985.

147. Willott, G.M. "Frequency of azoospermia." *For. Sci. Int.* 20:9–10, 1982.

148. Willot, G.M.; Allard, J.E. "Spermatozoa—their persistence after sexual intercourse." *For. Sci. Int.* 19:135–154, 1982.

149. Graves, H.C.B.; Sensabaugh, G.F.; Blake, E.T. "Postcoital detection of a male-specific semen protein." *NEJM.* 312:338–443, 1985.

150. Sensabaugh, G.F. Personal communication.

151. Silverman, E.F. "Persistence of spermatozoa in the lower genital tracts of women." *Am. J. Clin. Path.* 68:107, 1977.

152. Suzuki, O.; Oya, M.; Katsumata, Y.; et al. "A new enzymatic method for demonstrating choline in human seminal stains." *J. Forens. Sci.* 26:410–415, 1981.

153. ———. "A new enzymatic method for demonstrating spermine in human seminal stains." *J. Forensic Sci.* 25:99–102, 1980.

154. Parkin, B.H. "The evidential value of peptidase A as a semen typing system." *J. Forensic Sci.* 26:398–404, 1981.

155. Sensabaugh, G.F. "Isozymes in forensic science." Rattazzi, M.C.; Scandalios, J.G.; Whitt, G.S. (eds). *Isozymes: Current Topics in Biological and Medical Research.* New York, Alan R. Liss, Inc., volume 6. 247–282, 1982.

156. Race, R.R.; Sanger, R. *Blood Groups in Man.* Sixth edition. Oxford Blackwell, 1975.

157. Schulman, J. "The marital rape exemption in the criminal law." 14 *Clearinghouse Review.* 538–540, 1980.

158. Barry, S. "Spousal rape: The uncommon law." 66 *ABAJ*. 1088–1091, 1980.
159. Hilf, M.G. "Marital privacy and spousal rape." 16 *New England Law Review*. 31–44, 1981.
160. Griffin, M.K. "In 44 states it's legal to rape your wife." 9 *Student Lawyer*. 21–23, 57–61, 1980.
161. Blay-Cohen, S.; Coster, D.L. "Marital rape in California: for better or for worse." 8 *San Fernando Valley Law Review*. 239–261, 1980.
162. Morris, J.A. "The marital rape exemption." 27 *Loyola Law Review*. 597–610, 1981.
163. Letwin, L. " 'Unchaste Character,' ideology and the California rape evidence laws." 54 *Southern California Law Review*. 35–89, 1980.
164. Harris, L.R. "Toward a consent standard in the law of rape." 43 *University Chicago Law Review*. 613–645, 1976.
165. American Law Institute. "Model penal code and commentaries" (official draft and revised comments), article 213. The American Law Institute, Philadelphia, Penn., 1980.
166. Goodpaster, G. Associate Dean, School of Law, University of California, Davis. Personal communication.
167. Norvell, M.K.; Benrubi, G.I.; Thompson, R.J. "Investigation of microtrauma after sexual intercourse." *J. Reprod. Med.* 29:269–271, 1984.
168. Bassuk, E.L. "A crisis theory perspective on rape." In *The Rape Crisis Intervention Handbook*. McCombie, S.L. (Ed.). Plenum Press, New York. 121–129, 1980.
169. Notman, M.T.; Nadelson, C.C. "Psychodynamic and life-stage considerations." In *The Rape Crisis Intervention Handbook*. McCombie, S.L. (Ed.). Plenum Press, New York. 131–141, 1980.
170. McCombie, S.L.; Arons, J.H. "Counseling rape victims." In *The Rape Crisis Intervention Handbook*. McCombie, S.L. (Ed.). Plenum Press, New York. 145–171, 1980.
171. Silverman, D.; McCombie, S.L. "Counseling mates and families of rape victims. In *The Rape Crisis Intervention Handbook*. McCombie, S.L. (Ed.). Plenum Press, New York, 173–181, 1980.
172. Groth, A.N.; Birnbaum, H.J. "The rapist—motivations for sexual violence." In *The Rape Crisis Intervention Handbook*. McCombie, S.L. (Ed.). Plenum Press, New York. 17–26, 1980.
173. Burgess, A.W.; Holmstrom, L.L. "Rape typology and the coping behavior of rape victims." In *The Rape Crisis Intervention Handbook*. McCombie, S.L. (Ed.). Plenum Press, New York. 27–40, 1980.
174. Gill, P.; Jeffeys, A.J.; Werrett, O.J. "Forensic applications of DNA 'fingerprints.' " *Nature*. 318:S77–S79, 1985.
175. Giusti, A.; Baird, M.; Pasquale, S.; et al. "Application of de-oxyribonucleic acid (DNA) polymorphisms to the analysis of DNA recovered from sperm." *J. Forensic Sci.* 31:409–417, 1986.

176. Sensabaugh, G.F.; Blake, E.T.; Northey, D.H. "Genetic markers in semen III: Alteration of phosphoglucomutase isoenzyme patterns in semen contaminated by saliva." *J. Forensic Sci.* 25:470–478, 1980.

177. Brown, M.; Brown, C.G. "Specificity of two commercial acid phosphatase determination kits with respect to feminine hygiene products and vaginal contraceptives." *J. Forensic Sci.* 19:384–389, 1974.

178. Bashinski, J.S. "Detection of spermatozoa on vaginal swabs from victims of sexual assault: The ER versus the crime lab." Presented at the sixty-fifth semiannual seminar of the California Association of Criminalists. Oakland, Calif., May 1985.

179. Watt, K.W.K.; Lee, P.J.; M'Timkula, T.; et al. "Human prostate specific antigen: structural and functional similarity with serine proteases." *Proc. Matl. Acad. Sci.* USA 83:3166–3170, 1986.

180. Janerick, D.T.; Piper, J.M.; Glebatis, D.M. "Oral contraceptives and limb reduction defects." *NEJM.* 291:697–700, 1974.

181. Gal, I.; Kirman, B.; Stern, J. "Hormonal pregnancy tests and congenital malformations." *Nature.* 216:83, 1967.

182. Levy, E.P.; Cohen, A.; Fraser, F.C. "Hormone treatment during pregnancy and congenital heart defects." *Lancet.* 1:611, 1973.

183. Nora, J.J.; Nora, A.H. "Birth defects and oral contraceptives." *Lancet.* 1:941–942, 1973.

184. Rojas, F.J.; O'Conner, J.L.; Asch, R.H. "The antiprogesterone steroid RU-486 does not impair gonadotrapin-stimulated luteal adenyl cyclase activity or gonadotrapin release by pituitary cells." *J. Steroid Biochem.* 23(6A):1053–8, 1985.

185. Schindler, A.M.; Zanon, P.; Obradovic, D.; et al. "Early ultrastructural changes in RU-486 exposed decidua. *Gynecol. Obstet. Invest.* 20(2):62–7, 1985.

186. Vervest, H.A.; Haspels, A.A. "Preliminary results with the antiprogestational compound RU-486 (Miferpristone) for interruption of early pregnancy." *Fertil. Steril.* 44(5):627–32, 1985.

187. Kovacs, L.; Sas, M.; Resch, B.A.; et al. "Termination of very early pregnancy by RU-486—antiprogestational compound." *Contraception.* 29:399–410, 1984.

188. Shoupe, D.; Mishell, D.R.; Brenner, P.F.; Spitz, I.M. "Pregnancy termination with a high and medium dosage regime of RU-486." *Contraception.* 33(5):455–61, 1986.

189. Hodgen, G.D. "Pregnancy prevention by intravaginal delivery of a progesterone antagonist RU-486 for menstrual induction and absorbtion." *Fertil. Steril.* 44(2):263–7, 1985.

190. Rowlands, S.; Guilleband, J.; Bounds, W. "Side effects of danazol compared with an ethinylestradiol/norgestrel combination when used for postcoital contraception. *Contraception.* 27:39–49, 1983.

191. Martin, P.Y.; DiNitto, D.; Maxwell, S.; et al. "Controversies surrounding

the rape kit exam in the 1980s: Issues and alternatives." *Crime &* *Delinquency.* 31:223–246, 1985.

192. Antognoli-Toland, P. "Comprehensive program for examination of sexual assault victims by nurses: A hospital based project in Texas." *J. Emerg. Nursing.* 11:132–135, 1985.

193. DiNitto, D.; Martin, P.Y.; Norton, D.B.; et al. "After rape: Who should examine rape survivors?" *Am. J. Nursing.* May:538–540, 1986.

194. McCauley, J.; Guzinski, G.; Welch, R.; et al. "Toluidine blue in the corroboration of rape in the adult victim." *Am. J. Emerg. Med.* 5:105–108, 1987.

195. Lauber, A.; Souma G. "Use of toluidine blue for documentation of traumatic intercourse." *Obstet. Gynecol.* 60:644–646, 1982.

196. Laura X.; National Clearinghouse on Marital and Date Rape. Personal communication.

197. Higuchi, R.; von Beroldinger, C.H.; Sensabaugh, G.F.; Erlich, H.A. "DNA typing from single hairs." *Nature.* 332:543–546, 1988.

Index

About the Author

William M. Green completed his premedical education at the University of California, Berkeley, and graduated with a Bachelors Degree in Psychology. After receiving his doctorate of Medicine from Northwestern University, he completed a residency in Family Practice at the University of California, Davis Medical Center. Since 1977, he has been a faculty physician in the Division of Emergency Medicine and Clinical Toxicology at the University of California. Davis Medical Center. He is board certified in both family practice and emergency medicine. Since joining the Emergency Department, he has been involved in the care of hundreds of sexual assault victims. This experience and his interest in sexual assault has allowed him to serve as consultant to the Office of Criminal Justice Planning of the State of California.